HOW TO
ELIMINATE
NEGATIVE
Thinking

**Learn To Control Your Thoughts, Overthinking, Negativity Bias,
Heal Toxic Thoughts & Master Positive Self Talk & Self
Acceptance In Your Business & Personal Life**

Derek Borthwick

Dip.C.Hyp/NLP

DEDICATION

For Skye, Jamie and Adam.

"There is nothing either good or bad,
but thinking makes it so." - *William Shakespeare*

ABOUT THE AUTHOR

Derek Borthwick, *BSc. (Hons), Dip.C. Hyp/NLP*, is a multiple best selling author and leading mind expert. He has over thirty years of experience. Derek has worked with some of the world's largest companies and has lectured at top Scottish Universities. He specialises in advanced communication, persuasion and influence methods. Derek gained a diploma in clinical hypnotherapy and is a certified master practitioner of neuro linguistic programming (NLP). He also has a diploma in organisational and transformational coaching from the Henka Institute.

CONTENTS

PART ONE: The Mind Body Connection

PART TWO: Tools For Change

Bonus Rapid Learning Accelerator DTI Audio & Downloads At the End of Chapter 23

PREFACE

"To think is to be and to be is to think."

I've always been fascinated by human communication and interaction. Why do some people have such a positive outlook on life and others have a negative outlook? Are some people just born with a positive outlook while others are born with a negative outlook? This fascination led me deep into how the mind and brain work and what causes these different mental states. This has led to a lifetime of study and discovery. We all have negative thoughts from time to time together with self-doubts and we wouldn't be human if we didn't. However, it is the degree to which this affects our lives that can have a debilitating effect.

There are other books on eliminating negative thinking, but for me, there was always something missing. The missing parts to making the change complete. As a mind expert, this has led me to conclude that while tips are well intentioned, rarely do they work in isolation and that the real secret to any form of change lies deep within our minds. The very fact that you are reading this book would suggest that you have tried to solve this problem consciously. While a tip, such as going for a walk or meeting with a friend, can be a temporary solution, it doesn't address the underlying issue. Try giving a tip to someone who struggles with their weight and say: "Eat less and move more" and notice the reaction that you receive. We need simple methods and techniques to identify negative patterns of behaviour and to reduce, change and eliminate them.

I have never met anyone who is positive all the time. There have been difficult periods in my life that I had to overcome. I haven't always had a positive mental outlook. The difference now is that I have learned to control my thinking.

The encouraging news is that people who are negative thinkers actually have a talent and have hacked into their brains and their mind. They just have hacked into it in the wrong way! It is simply a matter of changing this to generate different results. This will become more apparent as we explore this further as we go through the book.

In this book, we are going to be exploring how our brains and minds work. We will draw on the scientific evidence and use some powerful technology to get you the results that you want. Simply working your way through this book and using it as a reference from now on will help to break down any previous negative patterns of thinking and ensure your success in the future. This will not only transform your business and professional life but also your personal, family and intimate relationships. We will combine both conscious and unconscious learning uniquely to balance your brain better.

The audio program will target the powerhouse of the unconscious mind to help program your mind for success. These methods and processes are very powerful and work. They will literally transform how you think. I truly believe that this is the most complete approach to eliminating negative thinking on offer.

HOW TO USE THIS BOOK

This book is divided into 2 parts.

Part One

Part one covers more of the theory and background to negative thinking, including how the brain, the nervous system and the mind work, together with an exploration of the origins of negative thinking including, belief, genetics versus environmental factors and the science of happiness.

Part Two

Part two builds on our new understandings and leverages the latest and most powerful methods to help eliminate negative thinking.

Your Bonus Audios

The real power lies within the unconscious mind. A specially recorded Rapid Learning Accelerator DTI Audio Program will help program your mind for success and is available to all readers **(See the end of Chapter 23).** It is recommended that you use earphones when listening to the tracks. The best time to use this recording is before going to sleep at night, or during a quiet period during the day when you will not be disturbed. Use the audio ideally once a day for 30 days.

There is also an additional bonus Total Body Relaxation Audio for you to download and listen to.

The Trip Is Not the Journey

There is a lot of information in this book. It is best to view this as an ongoing development plan. Make sure that you read the first part of the book carefully before moving on to the second part. The techniques discussed have the potential to change your thinking and, with it, your life. Let's make it fun. I'm excited to share this with you, so let's get started.

PART ONE

The Mind Body Connection

To Receive Your Complimentary Rapid Learning Accelerator DTI Audio and Bonus Total Body Relaxation Audio Go to the End of Chapter 23*

*These audios are very powerful. Do not use these tracks when driving, operating any machinery or when you need to be fully alert.

CHAPTER 1

What's Wrong?

My writings to date have been to help people better their business, personal and intimate lives. The bedrock of this relies on having the correct mental state. However, many of us may have slipped into negative thinking, and feel stuck in a sea of negativity, and feel that we are just not getting what we feel we deserve. This can cause a feeling of hopelessness and dissatisfaction with our lives and even depression. It can spill into and affect every part of our lives. Our internal machinery has let us down and yet no one teaches us how to fix it. We don't learn how our minds work at school and we are never given an instruction manual.

It is my passion to help people better themselves and fix this internal machinery. In this book, I have shared everything I possibly can to help you eliminate negative thinking and to get you back to your optimum mental state again. It is not just a book of tips, but a blueprint for success. The methods shared are very powerful and have helped millions of people, and they can help you, too.

At the same time, I realise that, depending on your level of negative thinking, there may be resistance to parts of the content. We are therefore going to incorporate the scientific evidence to help you come to your own conclusions. I would simply ask that you keep an open mind and if something works for you great, if not try something else. Try to resist the temptation to over analyse things. We don't question and want to know what all the wires are for when we drive our car or to know all the science behind manned flight. All we care about is will the car and plane get us to where we want to go?

The more that you can engage with the content and the exercises then the greater the extent of your success will be.

The Negative Trap

I would imagine that you're reading this book because you have concerns that negative thinking is impacting your professional, personal or intimate life. You may well have read books before or picked up some tips.

Some of these tips may have seemed encouraging and inspiring. However, frustration often sets in as people slip back into the same patterns of thinking as before. They are a slave to their thoughts having a lack of control over their negative thinking. This is because the part of the brain responsible for creating this has not been addressed. It is the powerhouse, and it runs over ninety-five per cent of what we do.

Often attempts to try harder fail and negative thinking patterns return a bit like a stretched elastic band snapping back into place. There is a reason for this, and a fresh approach is required. This book is unique because it uses an entire brain and mind approach, and leverages some of the most powerful techniques known. Your conscious mind does not know how to fix the problem. If it did, you would not be reading this book.

While I was writing this book, sitting at my desk, a bee flew into the room. The bee flew towards the window pane and continually kept bumping into it as it attempted to return outside. It would then rest for a while, move further along the window and try again. However, it would never be able to return to the outside again by doing this. It was doing the same thing over and over and was developing a habit. All the bee had to do was try something different. If it had simply turned around and flown out the way that it came in, it would have escaped.

It is the same with human behaviour and habits. We try the same thing consciously over and over again expecting different results. Einstein classed this as the definition of insanity. The problem is that our conscious mind is not the part of us that is creating the problem. It is not the one responsible for "powering the bus".

Repetition

In 2006, Neal et al. from Duke University estimated that habits account for around forty per cent of what we do. In addition, as much as ninety five per cent of what we experience is below conscious awareness. Many movements, gestures and postures have been performed thousands of times before. Think about interlocking your fingers. If I asked you which thumb was on top, most people would struggle to know the answer without actually performing the action. We can use this act of unconscious repetition of behaviours to help us to identify patterns of negative thinking that occur habitually.

Conscious Intervention

Your conscious mind can override some elements of negative thinking as long as it is paying attention. However, like the elastic band analogy mentioned earlier, negative thinking will snap back if manual intervention is not applied. Does this mean that a conscious approach will not work? It can, if repeated often enough, however, if we can engage both the unconscious mind and the conscious mind, then the likelihood of success is much greater.

The accompanying Rapid Learning Accelerator DTI Audio will speak to your unconscious mind and will accelerate the process. The changes will be subtle and will be below conscious awareness. I hope that you spot the irony that you will not notice the gradual change occurring. When used together with some of the other methods, this will help to ingrain new desirable behaviours. Details of where to find this are at the end of Chapter 23.

As we progress through this book, we're going to look at techniques that we can use to help eliminate negative thinking. Incorporating more than one technique can help speed up and solidify any change. This relates to the principle of stacking. In the same way that we can use stacking to build rapport, as discussed in earlier work, we can use it to eliminate negative thinking. Let's look at the principle of stacking to illustrate this.

The Stack

To illustrate this principle, I'm going to use a metaphor or example to help make it clearer. Imagine that I was to place a piece of paper on a table. The piece of paper on its own is pretty flimsy and if I were to blow on it, then it would move easily. However, if I then place another piece of paper on top of it, I have to blow slightly harder to move the paper. Eventually, when enough pieces of paper are placed on top of each other, the paper forms a rigid pile. It doesn't matter then how hard I blow on the pile of paper, it won't move.

The techniques and methods that will be shared with you represent pieces of paper. The more that we can stack different approaches on top of each other, then the more solid the solution is going to be.

DEFINING NEGATIVE THINKING

Let's begin by defining what we mean by negative thinking. This is the process where someone has a one sided or distorted view of an outcome and only sees the worst aspects. This includes dealing with people, situations, events, and expected outcomes. Someone who suffers from negative thinking always expects the worst in everything. Many people who engage in negative thinking often suffer from low self-esteem, low self-confidence and often depression. Negative thought patterns, if not corrected, can become habitual.

Someone who perpetually engages in negative thinking does not have balance in their thinking. Their thoughts are disproportionately represented by negative outcomes. Many people are unaware of just how negative they are or may appear. They are often oblivious to the impact that it has on those around them, together with their careers. Nobody likes to be around negative or miserable people. Often, negative thinking can be a protective mechanism. It stops people from being disappointed when things don't turn out the way they would like. We can't always get everything right one hundred per cent of the time. Even professional basketball players will miss baskets and professional soccer players will miss penalties.

Negative thoughts arise through the filtering mechanism in the brain, which we will explore in more detail later.

Another reason it can be so hard to escape this vicious cycle is that the anxiety feeds on our worst fears. You might have noticed that your negativity or overthinking is exacerbated by some specific triggers. These may be insecurities about personal capabilities, relationships with certain people, physical concerns, or mental health.

When people try to suppress their thoughts, when they are running out of control, this can often have the opposite effect. This causes even more overthinking and negativity.

Is Negativity Genetic?

Research into the causes of negativity is ongoing. There are competing theories. One theory suggests that it's a matter of personality and a trait inherited from our parents. It has been observed that certain groups, such as women, experience it more. However, is this genetic or environmental?

We see many times in the media that scientists have discovered a gene responsible for a particular behaviour. It then gets blown out of all proportion. However, as we dig deeper, we find out that it is not as straightforward as reported. We will explore this in greater detail in Chapter 9. The encouraging news from the field of epigenetics suggests your genes are not responsible for negative thinking.

We All Do It

Everybody engages in negative thinking. We wouldn't be human if we didn't. However, not everyone who engages in negative thinking has a mental illness, and not everyone who has a mental illness thinks negatively all the time. Research from the

National Science Foundation found that eighty per cent of our thoughts are negative, which suggests between about nine thousand to forty thousand negative thoughts a day.

A Bit of Negativity is Good

An element of negative thinking is useful and let's explore why. Imagine that we were standing on the top of a building. If I were to say to you: "Just jump off you will be fine", having negative thoughts about the consequences of this and its impact upon you would be useful. It gives us a sense of balance. If we just have a positive view of life for everything, then this does not give balance. We need negative thinking to experience positive thinking. Imagine that you took out a large loan without thinking about the consequences of not being able to make the payments. Having negative thoughts as part of an evaluation process is very useful. We don't want to erase all negative thinking, as it is part of our risk assessment. However, when this is not used for critique or evaluation but as the starting point for negativity and is continual, then there is an issue.

Somebody can't be useless or bad at everything and outcomes can't all be negative. Have you ever seen a person with a front and not a back? Rather, there is a sliding scale between the two points of bad and good. We need contrast to bring something into being. The problem with negative thinking is when it runs out of control like a runaway train. Someone may believe either in their own limitations or consider events and people conspiring against them in their life. The late Wayne Dyer once stated that he believed that people and life were conspiring against him, but positively! This is a great example of reframing, which we shall discuss later.

Negative thinking, and let's call it overly negative thinking or uncontrollable negative thinking, often relates to past events or worrying about future events. All memories are a lie, and all predictions of the future are a lie. Both are merely interpretations or predictions of what happened in the past or what may happen in the future. You may think that you knew what happened when recalling a memory as you experienced it. However, if all memories are the same, why do we recall them differently? Just ask somebody what they remember about a sports game or a movie to verify this. Try watching a movie for the second time. What did you miss the first time around?

When we look at how the brain interprets data, we will see that this is very rarely accurate. We are not aware of everything that is going on around us and we are only aware of a very small portion of what is occurring. We pay attention to only a small amount of the potential information that we can decode in our brains. For example, you are now aware of the feelings in your left foot and the clothing against your skin. This was occurring, but you were unaware of it. If I were to ask you to recall a memory of a few minutes ago, these particular sensations would have been unlikely to have been recalled. This is unless you had a pain in your left foot or clothing that was irritating your skin. We will explore this in greater detail when we look at the brain and mind.

Everything, therefore, is just an interpretation. It is your lie and peculiar to you. You may have heard the expression: "Are you a glass half full or half empty person"? Both of these statements are an interpretation of what you are seeing. A more correct statement is that the glass contains fifty per cent fluid and fifty per cent air.

13

We have established that we all have negative thoughts as we evaluate situations that we find ourselves in. Positive thinking has been advocated by many experts, and the health benefits associated with this have been well documented. That being said, it can be difficult to get out of the rut of negative thinking. Some people spend more time evaluating and thinking than others. For example, it is a good idea to appreciate the negative implications of not paying your mortgage or not paying your gas bill. These are normal things to evaluate or worry about. However, when thoughts become continual and intrusive and affect both our personal, business and intimate lives, then this needs addressing. This is particularly true when there is no substance to them.

Initially, negative thoughts may occur as isolated thoughts and then, with repetition, become a habit. If you are learning a new sport, then with practise, you will get better at it and ultimately you will become unconsciously competent. In other words, you don't know consciously how you do something, you just do it. The same is true of negative thinking. People who engage in negative thinking have a real talent. They have just learned to use it the wrong way. We will explore this later.

Let's move on now to what causes negative thinking.

CHAPTER 2

What Causes Negative Thinking?

Why do we have negative thoughts? Science suggests that when the amygdala (a part of the brain) becomes stimulated, it remains stimulated for a considerable time. The amygdala is one of two almond-shaped cell clusters located near the base of the brain in the limbic system. It is involved in emotion and memory and is connected to the fight-or-flight response. It responds to environmental threats and challenges and evaluates sensory information. Its main purpose is to regulate fear and aggression. It also attaches emotional meaning to memories, together with processing the reward system and decision-making processes.

Specific memories become paired with certain emotions. The stronger the emotion, the stronger the memory will be. The good news is that as you were responsible for laying down the memory in the first place, then you can change it. We will look at methods to do this in part two of the book.

We can learn to control our thoughts and the corresponding emotion. However, at times, certain thoughts can feel like they are like a runaway train and beyond our control. We also have to wrestle with the inner voice, which is often critiquing us and passing negative comments. These thoughts and the inner voice can take us away from what is happening in the present, and very often we miss out on the pleasure of the moment.

Many of us have an assumption that we should be happy all the time. When things go against us, the more we dwell on these events, the emptier and more despondent we become. Our thoughts can make us or destroy us. We will look at how they literally can kill us in Chapter 7. For now, though, we are reminded of the quote at the beginning of the book.

"There is nothing either good or bad, but thinking makes it so"

-William Shakespeare

EFFECTS OF NEGATIVE THINKING

Severe cases of negative thinking can cause depression, sadness, lethargy, and emptiness. Negative thinking can arise from depression, leading to in extreme cases, suicide. Other conditions associated with negative thinking are panic attacks and obsessive compulsive disorder (OCD). OCD is categorised as an anxiety condition. Even though OCD sufferers know that their thinking is irrational, they still find it difficult to control their behaviour. Such is the power of the unconscious mind which we will learn about.

CAUSES OF NEGATIVE THINKING

Fear of the Future

Fear of the future and anxiety about the current circumstances or events can cause negative thinking. Some may feel that time is slipping away from them. Many worry about not achieving everything that they had hoped to do in their lives. Others suffer from "imposter syndrome" and we will address this later. This can lead to feelings of anxiety and despair. If this is not addressed, it can affect mental and physical health.

Fear of the Past

Another cause of negative thinking is feeling anxious about past events. Some people ruminate on past failures and opportunities missed. This often leads to self-criticism, which can enhance negativity.

Physical Origins

Feelings of negativity can sometimes result from a physical disorder or personal image. Lack of sleep or an illness can lead to negative thinking. Mood, well-being and self-identity can all be severely affected.

The Challenges

Overcoming negative thinking patterns is not as easy as most people think. Just try telling someone who struggles with their weight to eat less and move more and see the reaction that you get! The key is to have a genuine desire to overcome negative thinking. Simply following the techniques and methods listed in this book means you can start on a remarkable transformation. They are your thoughts, and you can learn to control them.

Patterns of Negativity

Much of what we do in everyday life is unconscious repetitions of patterns of behaviour. Psychologists have estimated that up to ninety-five per cent of what we do one day will be repeated the next. Repeated patterns of behaviour can be described as habits.

Habits can be both good and bad and can be useful. They are unconscious patterns of learned behaviour. We wouldn't want to have to re-learn every day how to brush our teeth. They can however, be destructive. There are four stages of learning that we will learn about in Chapter 5.

If you are constantly engaging in negative thinking in the form of images, feelings, or internal dialogue, then this can become habitual. It is just as easy to learn a bad habit as a useful one. We can train our brains to engage in negative thinking. Remember, be careful what you ask for, it may not be what you want!

Habits, however, can be changed. In some cases, this can be challenging, but people always have choices. Someone who stopped smoking always has that ability to start again. However, as a new pattern of non smoking behaviour becomes more ingrained, then it becomes more difficult to return to the previous pattern of smoking again.

Will Power Alone?

Eliminating negative thinking just by using "willpower" alone can be challenging. Let's use a rubber band as a metaphor to illustrate this.

Imagine that you had a large rubber resistance band tied around your waist. You may have seen some of these at the gym and they provide resistance when training. Let's assume that the band can be stretched and broken, but only if a lot of force is supplied. When the band is not taut, it's easy to start walking. However, the more you move away then the more the rubber band stretches and the more resistance it provides. Ultimately, you end up being pulled back. We have to use willpower and force to resist the band. Willpower is not constant and is dependent on several variables, including blood glucose levels. The reader is referred to the book by Roy F Baumeister and John Tierney "Willpower" for more information. After a while, you may become tired or fed up. You are either pulled back by the band or you push forward and break free.

Patterns of behaviour are similar to the resistance band. Think about the conscious mind as representing you when you walk forward and the band becomes taut. As long as you keep pressure on that band, you won't get pulled back. However, as soon as your attention is diverted elsewhere or you're not concentrating, it will snap you straight back. Ideally, we want to break the resistance band so that it can't snap us back.

In this book, we are going to be exploring many techniques to give choice. Some may challenge your current thinking and be "eye-opening". I would urge that you suspend disbelief and just go along with what you are discovering. By the end of this book, you may well have a different view of the world and yourself. Try to have an open mind and just go with the flow.

CONTROLLING NEGATIVE THINKING

Reducing negative thoughts and establishing greater positive thinking enhances mental wellbeing. This provides a better, more balanced perception of the world to us.

Health Benefits

The adverse effects of excessive stress on our well-being have been well documented. However, small amounts are useful for us. Work in 2016, by Kaufer, Kirby, and colleagues at the University of California, discovered that some stress on occasion can actually help us. Studies on rats showed that acute, short-lived stress doubled the creation of new neurons in the hippocampus. The hippocampus is the part of the brain responsible for laying down memories. A small amount of stress can be good. If there wasn't any stress, there wouldn't be any motivation to do anything. It's the balance of stress that is important in our lives and the ability to control unwanted stress that matters.

Argue for Your Weakness and It's Yours

Negative thinking often comes from comparing ourselves to others and their achievements, together with perceived limitations in our abilities. Comparing against other people is always futile as there is always someone richer or more successful than us.

There are different measurements of success. Not every part of everyone's life is perfect. Those considered as being financially successful may have health issues or family problems. We can't control other people's success, but we can control ourselves and our perceptions.

Party On

Imagine that we had been at a party and had too much to drink. We may have said or done something and then woken up in the morning feeling paranoid. The entire event is often blown out of proportion. Often when we speak to someone about the incident, they have not even noticed or remembered it.

Do You Remember?

People have surprisingly short memories and cannot retain information easily. Let's imagine that you watched a soap opera or a sports game on television last night. If I was to ask you the next day what happened in the game or on the television show, you would probably be able to recall a fair proportion of it. If I was to ask you a week later, your memory probably starts to get hazier. If I were to ask you a month down the line, you would struggle to remember anything unless something monumental happened in the episode or the game.

Something that we may worry over and remember vividly will soon be long forgotten about by others. Today's newspapers are tomorrow's rubbish or trash.

SELF-LIMITING BELIEFS

Many of us may be convinced that we can't do something. One of my favourite quotes is by Henry Ford:

"Whether you think that you can or think that you can't, you're right."

Let's look at an example to illustrate this.

Walking the Plank

Imagine that I was to place a plank of wood on the ground with a width of 24 inches or 60 centimetres. If you are able-bodied and I was to ask you to walk across that plank of wood, you could probably do it relatively easily in most cases.

Now let's assume that I take the same plank of wood and raise it in the air. This time I place it between two buildings three storeys up and ask you to walk across the plank of wood. Now it gets tricky. Many of you may say that you could not do it. Yet earlier you were more than capable of walking across the same plank of wood when it was placed on the ground. What has changed? It is the context that has changed. When the plank is raised into the air, your brain has now assessed more variables and has assessed what could happen if things went wrong. Yet the very act of walking across the plank of wood from a physical point of view is exactly the same. In this case, having some negative thoughts would be useful as there is danger associated with it. However, many people take the same level of negative thinking and apply this to walking across the plank while it is on the ground!

Mental Disorders

A large proportion of the population is trapped in negativity due to mental disorders. Anyone can suffer from a mental illness, and many of us have had times in our lives when we have struggled with our mental wellbeing.

It is important to be honest with ourselves and to seek professional help if this has been a long-standing issue. The techniques in this book have solid foundations, are very powerful, and are used by many professionals as part of therapy. They will work for most people if applied correctly. However, if you are in any doubt, I would urge you to seek professional help. There is nothing to be embarrassed or frightened about. If you suffered a fall and had a serious injury, you would immediately seek a Doctor would you not? Look after your mind as you would your body.

This book is primarily designed for those who have slipped into negativity or who suffer from negative thinking but are not completely debilitated or paralysed by it.

Don't Ignore It

Many people ignore negative thoughts in the hope that they will go away. Some have developed strategies to deal with negative thinking. Others distract themselves or keep themselves busy, either through work or hobbies. Some have resorted to pharmaceutical drugs, alcohol and or narcotics. These methods are crutches and they're a bit like putting a plaster on a deep wound, only a temporary solution.

The first step is accepting and acknowledging these thoughts for what they are. You are not a negative thinker you are a person having negative thoughts. Repeat these statements and notice the different feelings associated with each one.

"I am a negative thinker."

"I am a person having negative thoughts."

Being a negative thinker is a state of being. It is not who you are.

INCONSISTENT THINKING

Do we think rationally, or do we jump to conclusions? Let's start with a little puzzle to find out? The aim here is not to try and solve the puzzle, but to listen to your intuition.

The Puzzle

A bat and ball cost $1.10.

The bat costs one dollar more than the ball.

How much does the ball cost?

When you did this calculation, a number probably came into your mind. That number may have been $0.10 and for many of us, we would be convinced that it is the right number.

It seems an easy puzzle, and yet $0.10 is the wrong answer. Surely not. If you do the calculation again, you will see the correct answer. Let's go through it again. If the ball costs $0.10, then the bat and ball will cost $1.20, which is $0.10 for the ball and $1.10 for the bat and not $1.10. The correct answer is therefore $0.05.

Even if you did get the answer correct, it is most likely that you managed to resist the intuitive answer of $0.10. When I first heard this puzzle, I had to think long and hard about it to get the correct answer. I too incorrectly said the cost of the ball was $0.10.

Psychologists have been interested in thinking systems that humans use. Keith Stanovich and Richard West, identified two systems in the mind, System 1 and System 2.

System 1 operates automatically and quickly, with little or no effort and without voluntary control.

System 2 allocates attention to the task, including complex computations. The operations of System 2 are often associated with the subjective experience of availability, choice, and critical thinking. The following examples are taken from "Thinking Fast and Slow" by Daniel Kahneman.

Examples of Fast Thinking System 1

1. Detecting that one object is more distant than another.
2. Turning towards the source of a sudden sound.
3. Completing the phrase "bread and...".
4. Making a facial expression of disgust when shown a horrible picture.

5. Detecting hostility in a voice.
6. Answering 2 + 2 =
7. Reading words on large billboards.
8. Driving a car on autopilot without thinking.
9. Understanding simple sentences.

Examples of Slow Thinking System 2

1. Focusing your attention on one member of a live rock band.
2. Focusing on the voice of one person in a crowded and noisy room.
3. Looking for a woman with red hair.
4. Searching your memory to identify a surprising sound.
5. Maintaining a faster walking speed than is natural for you.
6. Self-analysing your behaviour in a social situation.
7. Comparing two items for overall value.
8. Filling out a complex form.
9. Checking the validity of a complex logical argument.

For Slow Thinking System 2, we must pay attention to perform well. When people intensely focus on a task, they can become blind to what else is going on.

Christopher Chabris and Daniel Simons in their book The Invisible Gorilla shot a short film of two teams passing a basketball between them. One team was wearing white shirts while the other was wearing black shirts. The viewers were asked to count the number of passes made by the white team and to ignore the passes made by the black team.

Halfway through the video, a woman wearing a gorilla suit appears and crosses the court and begins thumping her chest before moving on. The gorilla is in view for around nine seconds.

Thousands of people have seen the video and about half of them did not notice anything unusual. It is the introduction of counting that causes the blindness. I witnessed this myself first hand when I went to see the British illusionist Derren Brown. He conducted a similar experiment and filmed it while doing so. He asked the audience if they had noticed anything unusual. There were only a few people in the audience who noticed the gorilla. I wasn't one of them! I was too busy counting the number of passes. Magicians know that the narrower the focus of attention and the more that somebody concentrates then the less they see of what is going on around them. It is the person who is not paying attention and who is in the periphery of the group that can cause a problem for a magician.

The gorilla study illustrates two important facts about our minds namely, that we can be blind to the obvious, and we are also blind to our blindness.

Our Distorted System 1

To show the power of the fast thinking system one, take a look at Fig. 1 below.

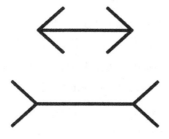

Fig.1

When we look at the figure, we can see that the line at the top is shorter than the line at the bottom. However, if you measure both lines, you will see that they are of an identical length. This is known as the Müller-Lyer illusion.

Our senses and with it our perceptions are often manipulated by external events and don't represent what is really going on or what has happened.

Imagine that you meet somebody for the first time at a party called "Dave" and you find him easy to talk to. Later on, someone at the party then asks you if you know of anyone who might wish to contribute towards their fund raising. You think of Dave, even though the only thing you know about him is that you found him easy to talk to. Our brains extrapolate and assume that because we found him easy to talk to, that we would like everything else about him. We are often suspicious or disapprove of people that we know little about.

When we oversimplify things without sufficient information, this often leads to judgment errors. This is called exaggerated emotional coherence and is also known as the "Halo" effect. This can work in reverse too.

We also have other cognitive biases, including confirmation bias. This is the tendency for people to agree with arguments and information that supports their current beliefs and to accept whatever information is suggested to them. Confirmation bias is such a powerful bias and exists throughout human interactions, and even science is not immune to it. In many cases science can suffer from the dogma that has resulted from habitual thinking and confirmation bias. Whenever something is a challenge to our criteria and values and our map of the world, then this becomes harder to change, particularly if somebody tries to force it upon us.

Snap decisions occur beneath our level of awareness and occur unconsciously. We often find ourselves in situations where we have to make quick judgments. Our minds have developed shortcuts to help us, and these are called heuristics. In most cases, these are very useful. For example, we don't want to have to learn every day that putting our hand in the fire causes us to be burnt. While useful, our mind tends to overuse them and this can lead to making mistakes.

Guess what the words say in Fig.2 below.

JUMPING TO CONCLUSIONS

Fig.2

Turn over the page and see if you are correct. Let's look at some examples of heuristics.

The first one is a substitution heuristic, and this is where we answer an easier question than the one that was actually posed. When we put this in the context of negative thinking, we are not answering the questions that we posed to ourselves logically. If we ask ourselves why this always happens to us, then often, we will provide a simpler answer to this question than the question is seeking. The answer may be: "Because we are useless". However, it is impossible to be "useless" at everything.

Then there is the example of an availability heuristic. This is where you overestimate the probability of something that you hear often or find easy to remember. Let's look at an example. Strokes cause many more deaths than accidents. However, one study found that eighty per cent of respondents thought that accidental death was more likely than a stroke. This is because accidental deaths have been reported more in the media and because they make a stronger impression on us. We remember horrific events more readily.

To stop us from coming to illogical conclusions, it is worth providing a base rate. The numbers don't lie, but people do, often unintentionally. It is difficult to apply a baseline to negative thinking, so we must sharpen our awareness and ask: "Is what we are thinking logical?" Let's use an example to illustrate this.

Lies Dam Lies & Statistics

Let's use a very simple example to illustrate how our thinking can be skewed. Imagine that I had a coin in my hand and I tossed it up and it came down heads up. Suppose that I tossed the coin another four times and in each case it came down heads up. You now have to place a bet on the next toss and select whether it is more likely to be a head or a tail.

Did you select a tail? Many of us feel that because there have been five previous heads, that it must be more likely that we're going to have a tail. However, each toss is independent and not contingent on the previous toss. This means that in every case when a coin is tossed there is a fifty per cent chance of heads and a fifty per cent chance of tails.

We see our thinking can be skewed. This is not just confined to statistics, as we can use the same flawed logic when we are thinking about something negatively. "Why does this always happen to me?" "I never seem to get the opportunities." "There is not much point in me applying for the job, as I didn't get the last one." The brain is very good at skewing information and your unconscious mind will do its best to give you what you ask for, which may not be what you want. Below is the answer to the question asked previously relating to Fig.2.

IUMRING TQ GQNGIUSIQNS

Our thinking is not consistent and will vary depending on many factors. Research has found that judges are more likely to grant parole at the beginning of the day or after a food break than immediately before such a break. If judges are hungry, the sentences they issue are tougher.

A separate study of thousands of juvenile court decisions found that judges' decisions are influenced by whether the local football team loses a game on the weekend. If they do, then harsher decisions are made on the Monday following the weekend. Another study, which looked at one and a half million judicial decisions over three decades, found that judges are tougher on days that follow a loss by the local city's football team than they are on days that follow a win.

Bizarrely enough, birthdays can affect a judge's decisions. In a study of six million decisions made by judges in France over twelve years, it was found that defendants are given more leniency on their birthday!

Judges are not immune to the effects of the weather, it appears. The outside temperature has been shown to influence judges. A review of 207,000 immigration court decisions over four years found that when it is hot outside, people are less likely to get asylum.

If professionals who are paid for their ability to critically evaluate can have their thinking be so easily influenced, don't be too hard on yourself when external factors affect your decisions.

In the next chapter, we will look at some different types of negative thinking.

CHAPTER 3

Types of Negative Thinking

We have discussed negative thinking, its effects, symptoms, and causes in the previous chapter. There is little point in going into all potential subcategories related to negative thinking, as most people want a solution and not a label. However, before we move onto a deeper understanding of how humans are wired, it is worth covering three specific forms of negative thinking that are commonplace. These are imposter syndrome, rumination and overthinking. Let's clarify what these are.

IMPOSTER SYNDROME

Imposter syndrome was first documented in high-achieving women in the 1970s. While imposter syndrome is still more prevalent among women, men are also prone to developing this mindset.

People who suffer from imposter syndrome have a belief that they don't deserve their achievements and the high esteem in which they are held. Inwardly, they feel as if they aren't, as they are perceived by others. Many competent or intelligent people consider themselves undeserving. They feel that eventually they will be found out and people may discover the real truth about them. People who suffer from imposter syndrome often feel like frauds. This may be the case even though they are highly academically qualified and may hold a high office or a very senior position. Even with evidence to the contrary, people suffering from imposter syndrome often put down their achievements to luck, good fortune, or good timing.

How common is imposter syndrome?

It has been estimated that approximately thirty per cent of those suffering from imposter syndrome are high achievers. However, it is not just restricted to high achievers. Research suggests that as much as seventy per cent of adults may experience imposter syndrome at least once during their life.

RUMINATION

Rumination is another form of negative thinking and involves repetitive, excessive thoughts. It can interfere with other types of thinking and can be self-consuming. It is often associated with conditions such as obsessive-compulsive disorder (OCD) and general anxiety. However, many of us not suffering from a diagnosed disorder engage in this type of thinking from time to time. Rumination starts as the mind begins to dwell on certain thoughts and feelings of fear. This can result in anxiety and helplessness can take over. Thoughts associated with rumination include reflection and brooding.

Reflection

Reflection can be a useful part of rumination as long as it does not get out of control. It allows us to think about certain aspects. It provides context to the powerful emotions that are associated with the experience.

Brooding

Brooding results from dwelling on the feeling of helplessness either from an event that has already happened, or concerns about future events. Emotions of hopelessness can result often from stress accompanying it.

Sometimes people replay a mental movie which has an accompanying narrative. This might be recalling an event or imagining a certain outcome or future. Very often, this mental movie, internal voice, or feeling keeps replaying and looping back on itself.

Many people who are brooding may be trying to solve a problem or to stop a particular event from reoccurring. Some are seeking validation and justification from a particular event or behaviour.

Causes of Rumination

Rumination can be triggered by certain triggers and by obsessively recalling a particular event, behaviour or situation. Many of us engage in rumination from time to time. If, for example, we know that we have to deliver a talk in front of people, this may cause fear as we think of all the things that may go wrong.

We may have suffered a relationship breakup. This can result in thinking obsessively about this as we replay all the things that we might have done differently. In most cases, these thoughts will disappear with time, however, there are strategies that we can use to accelerate the removal of this type of thinking. We will explore these later in this book.

If thoughts continue to linger and become permanent, this can indicate mental health issues and professional advice should be sought.

OVERTHINKING

Overthinking, unlike regular thinking, causes you to dwell on a problem without the aim of establishing a solution. Thinking deeply as part of a self-reflection process can be useful, as you can discover insights about yourself.

To keep it simple, self-reflection leads to useful insights, whereas overthinking does not have a solution focus. If you are engaging in overthinking, the first step to do is to become aware of it. Some examples of overthinking include thinking about a negative event in your past, and over analysing every detail. We may also engage in over analysing our everyday interactions with other people. There are many other examples that we could list, but the key thing to become aware of is when it is happening and to develop a strategy to deal with it.

When aware of overthinking, it is useful to take the role of an independent observer and notice what effect this thinking pattern is having on your emotional and body sensations. Think of this as like being at a movie theatre and observing yourself on the screen.

Too much overthinking can cause an excessive inward focus at the expense of experiencing our external reality. Many people have missed out on many of life's important experiences from having their minds elsewhere.

Sometimes negative thinking and overthinking haunts us because we have set expectations that far exceed our abilities. Setting overly high or unrealistic goals can result in disappointment, feelings of guilt, anger, anxiety, depression and self-blame. To help overcome these problems, goal setting needs to be realistic and we will cover goal setting in Part Two, together with its benefits.

Triggers

Emotional triggers often start the process of overthinking. It is useful to identify and understand these emotional triggers. Words, opinions, situations and even the very presence of another person can act as a trigger.

The stronger the trigger and the negative emotion, then the stronger the pattern of overthinking. Triggers are referred to as anchors and can be initiated through our senses. This can be in the form of an image, sound, touch, taste, or an internal feeling. We will look at the scientific evidence for how these triggers have been "anchored" in Chapter 20.

Beliefs, Criteria & Values

Most of us defend and adhere to our belief systems. These have been learned and set down and form the basis of our lives. We will resist what we think of ourselves, what others think about us, and what we believe to be true. People tend to prefer a comfortable lie to an uncomfortable truth.

Choice of Language

Pay attention to these three sentences and notice how they make you feel when you say them:

"I am an unsuccessful person."

"I'm a person who has not achieved success."

"I am a person who has not achieved success, yet."

The first statement is a statement of being. This is not who you are and what does "unsuccessful" mean? It is an adjective, and any meaning is subjective. Let's explore this.

If you can get up in the morning and dress yourself, then this is successful. If you can drive a car, then this is a successful activity. We need to drill a bit more down into what being unsuccessful means? Be very wary when you hear adjectives and adverbs because they have no meaning other than the subjective meaning that somebody attaches to them. For example:

"The car was driving slowly down the road."

What does this actually mean? It means different things to different people. Was the car driving at three miles per hour or kilometres per hour? Perhaps it was driving at 10 miles per hour or kilometres per hour. We don't know and have to attach our meaning to the adjective or adverb.

People will often make generalised statements too. Negative thoughts may include, for example, someone going on a date and getting stood up. They may say:

"I always get stood up."

This statement is unlikely to be true. When you hear the internal voice and it's speaking in generalisations, be aware of it. Also, if you find yourself using generalisations when speaking to other people, start becoming aware of this. It is often beneficial to write things down, as it encourages us to be specific.

Our unconscious mind does not think and take things literally. If you say that you are an unsuccessful person and you are referring to a particular activity, then your unconscious mind will make sure that there is no cognitive dissonance. It will do its best to match what you believe to be true, and this may mean making sure that you are unsuccessful. We tend to get what we ask for, which may not be what we want.

We touched on the unconscious mind in this chapter. We will explore the mind in more detail in Chapter 5. Next, let's move on to the biology of fear.

Before we do, this book contains many of the most powerful methods to help eliminate negative thinking. However, for those that are looking for some additional help and a fast-track method, I have recorded the special *Rapid Learning Accelerator* audio tracks series, which includes:

"Be More Positive"

&

"Supreme Confidence"

These audio programs specifically target the unconscious mind. This will help reprogram your mind for success. If this is of interest, these are available from:

https://www.power2mind.com/-nlp-audio

You do not need to purchase these to get the most from this book. These are designed for people who want some extra help beyond what I share in this book.

To receive a 70% reader's discount on these audio programs, please use the code Power70.

CHAPTER 4

The Biology of Fear

What is it that causes negativity, nervousness, and anxiety? Scientists believe that we are only born with two fears. These are the fear of loud noises and the fear of falling. This would imply that all other fears have been learned. Negative thinking often comes about from a fear of failure. This may also arise from not being able to do something or somebody not liking us. We may feel someone does not like what we are doing or stand for.

There is a useful acronym that corresponds to the letters FEAR. It is, *"future events appearing real"* or *"future expectations appearing real"*. We will look at reality and imagination in more detail in the next chapter when we look at the brain and mind.

In chapter 2, we saw that by raising a plank of wood in the air, that the context changes. The perception of the difficulty of walking along the plank increased even though the physical activity was the same. What happened? Our fear response was triggered and the protective mechanism kicked in as the brain attempted to protect us. The brain identified that there is a possibility that if we were to fall, we could either be killed or seriously injured. This stimulates the part of the autonomic nervous system responsible for stress. If we do not control this, then we have a runaway state, and panic can set in.

People who get nervous and enter a runaway state have a talent for using their imagination. They have just learned to use this talent in the wrong way!

A Real PEAR?

The past and present, as we have discussed, are mere illusions and are not accurate representations of what happened or what could happen. In the same way that we can use the acronym "FEAR" to express future events appearing real, we can also use the acronym "PEAR" which stands for past events appearing real.

Remember, memories are a lie and even history is just a lie agreed upon. It is just someone's interpretation of events. Have you ever been to a sports game and discussed the team or an individual's performance with someone? It may be that the other person is convinced that their team should have won, even though the consensus opinion is that they should have lost.

Have you ever watched a movie with a friend or partner and they mentioned something that they observed in the movie and you didn't see it? The same thing happens when you see a movie the second time around. The second time around, we often notice things that we didn't spot the first time.

How many things may have occurred related to you that were positive that you filtered out and ignored?

You may at this point be questioning this, and it will become clearer when we explore how our brains and minds work later. First, let's look at our nervous system.

TWO NERVE CENTRES

We have an autonomic nervous system that runs below our conscious awareness. Within this autonomic nervous system, there are two systems responsible for regulating the organs of the body in response to a stimulus (Fig.4). There is the parasympathetic nervous system and the sympathetic nervous system. The hypothalamus in the brain maintains homeostasis or balance between the two nervous systems.

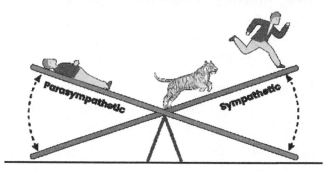

Homeostasis Is the Balance Between the Parasympathetic and Sympathetic Nervous System.

Rest, Heal and Digest – Parasympathetic Nervous System Stimulated

Fight, Flight or Freeze – Sympathetic Nervous System Stimulated

Fig.4

The parasympathetic nervous system is stimulated when we are at rest, "the rest and digest state". The sympathetic nervous system is stimulated by the fear response at times of stress. When stressed, the amygdala sends a message to the hypothalamus. If overstimulated, it triggers the fight, flight, or freeze response. This prepares the body for fight or flight by increasing the blood flow to the large muscles and away from the extremities. Breathing becomes shallower, faster, and higher in the chest and the heart rate increases. Non-essential systems shut down and peripheral vision together with hearing are reduced. We experience tunnel or foveal vision. The digestive and immune systems also shut down. This results in butterflies in the stomach. Now that we know what happens when somebody is stressed or nervous, we will see this manifest itself in the body's outward expression.

When in the resting stage, blood flow to the extremities is increased. This can cause a flushed look on the face, a fuller lower lip and deeper and slower breathing. The pupils will be less dilated to allow for a wider field of view. If shaking hands with someone, the hand is often warm and not moist.

Compare this to someone that is nervous or stressed and there will be less colour in their face. The language reflects this with the expression "white as a ghost". The breathing is also shallower and higher in the chest, and the lower lip is less full and paler. The hands are often cold to the touch and may be moist too. You may detect "bad breath" as the person is in ketosis.

Acting Stressfully

You may have had a situation where you have either been in a heated debate or argument or when somebody was shouting at you. You may not have been able to think of what to say and your voice may have tensed up. You may even have said some odd things. Then afterwards, as you calm down, you may have thought to yourself: "I wish I had said that," as you replay the argument over again in your mind. Most people feel like that. This is nothing to worry about.

What has happened? Blood drained from the prefrontal cortex, shutting down the critical function. When this occurs, it

41

makes it virtually impossible to learn anything or to focus on small things. It also makes it difficult to engage with other people. The survival instinct kick in and this affects our inability to remember things. Many of us will have had the experience of being under stress and trying to read a page in a book. We can read a passage repeatedly and it just won't go in. Why does this happen? This is because our critical brain has shut down.

Thoughts that Hang About

After an argument is long over, we think about all the things that we could have said but didn't. The time associated with these strong emotions is called the "Emotional Refractory Period" (ERF).

It shifts our perceptual filters to make us focus only on what conforms to our current emotion. When in an ERP, a person seeks very hard to confirm their beliefs rather than challenge them. There is little point in trying to provide evidence to the contrary that shows that the person is wrong. The strength of emotions stimulated during the ERP is so strong that people will not be able to accept the idea of being wrong.

After Effects

If an ERP goes beyond a few hours or days, then perception can be distorted. If allowed to linger, then ERPs can lead to distorted worldviews that are seldom useful.

If you are upset and not responding appropriately, don't blame yourself. Most people in an ERP act in the same way. It is best to allow someone who is in a state of anger to calm down until the ERP has settled down. If not, there is a risk that the person will go back into the original state. Understanding that an ERP is taking place helps us to understand how to manage our emotions better.

We will explore this in more detail when we look at how the brain and mind work.

You Do It to Yourself

We may hear comments such as "she drives me crazy!" This is incorrect. Someone else does not make us feel bad. We do this to ourselves by choosing how we react to a situation.

Where's the Instruction Manual?

There is more to controlling our thinking than at first thought. Imagine that you had just been given a new piece of electrical equipment or have downloaded some software for your computer. If there was no instruction manual, then we have to learn by trial and error. We might never work it out and may never discover the shortcuts. Many of us use our computers daily without realising that there are shortcuts. It's not until we search for a quicker method or until someone shows us some shortcuts to make it easier that we learn it. How much better would it be if we had a simple manual with shortcuts?

Think about our brains and minds. As we enter the world, nobody says: "*Welcome to the world and here is your instruction manual*". We try various things and make lots of mistakes along the way. Some of us never truly master the workings of the brain and mind. Think about how much easier it would be if an instruction manual had been given to us. How useful would that have been?

Your Talent

Depending on your belief system and your ability to become immersed in either a past or future memory will depend on how you respond. People who can become heavily absorbed in negative thinking simply through imagination have a talent. It just needs to be trained in the correct way.

For some people, their imagination is so good that even the thought of fingernails being scraped against a blackboard or imagining the squeaking sound of hands being rubbed against balloons can cause severe discomfort. Some people, with a fear of heights, can feel uncomfortable from watching video footage of someone on the edge of a cliff. If this is you, then you have a great imagination. It is comforting to know that Einstein said:

"Imagination is more important than knowledge."

Emotional Not Logic

Human beings are emotional creatures. Everything a human being does is in response to an emotion or a feeling. In the author's earlier works, "How to Talk to Anybody", & "Body Language How to Read Any Body", a strong psychological link was established between the inner thoughts and the outer expression. We may think that we are logical however, our decisions are governed by emotions and justified by some form of logic.

For the brain to believe something is true, it doesn't have to be true, it just has to be plausible. If you are engaged in negative thinking and saying to yourself that you could never deliver a talk or speak in front of a group of people, then this is an emotionally generated response. You may remember a time in the past when you had a bad experience and use this to justify your reasoning. This gives an element of critical evaluation and logic to the emotion that you just had. However, is it true?

How Many Times Do You Say It?

I remember hearing a quote from David Lee Roth, the front man of the legendary rock band Van Halen, who said:

> *"If you tell someone often enough how good you are in the end, they will believe you."*

This doesn't just have an effect when saying this to other people, it also has an effect when we say this to ourselves too. If we constantly repeat the same message in the form of negative self-talk, negative images, or negative emotions, then this will also affect us. Have you ever told somebody a white lie? If you have, you may then find yourself repeating that lie to other people, and after a while, it then feels true.

Our emotions are powerful generators. We either move towards pleasure or move away from pain. People are not wholly in one camp or the other but can switch between the two and this is context driven. Someone may be very motivated to generate new revenue for their business but has low motivation to fill in their tax return. They fill in the latter to avoid the pain of any consequences.

Getting Emotional

People act according to the principle "WIIFM" which is, "what's in it for me". You may think that this is not true. Perhaps you know or may have come across, altruistic or unselfish people. However, everything humans do is in response to a feeling. They either want to get more of a feeling or less of a feeling.

Think about when you give money to someone who is homeless or you give to a charity. Why do you do it? The logical part of your brain reasons that you do this to help other people. However, what emotion do you get when you do this? How do you feel? For most people, it makes them feel good, and that's why they do it. Such is the driving force behind the need to satisfy our emotions that this can result in unusual or bizarre logic and behaviour at times. These emotions are generated unconsciously. We can see this with people who are hypnotised. They can be persuaded to do things that are quite out of character.

The act of negative thinking, while frustrating for the individual, can be a result of the unconscious mind attempting to protect you. Imagine that you are in a job and that you are having negative thoughts and worrying that you may be made redundant or being let go from your job. This is a valid concern, and some negativity or worry is helpful. If you detect that things are not quite right at your place of work, then you can take action to address this. You can either improve your performance or look for another job. It is when this thought becomes all-consuming and not based on evidence, but is "worry for worry's sake" that problems can arise. The more often that this becomes repeated, the more it becomes perceived and accepted as a "truth".

There is a lot of scientific evidence to show that belief affects the outcome, so be very careful what you wish for it might just come true. This can become a self-fulfilling prophecy. If it does, then your brain satisfies itself that it was correct all along. The unconscious mind takes things literally and if you keep telling yourself that you're going to be made redundant, then your unconscious mind will do its best to help to make this a reality.

You may find yourself making more errors at work, or perhaps your communication skills slip, and your interaction with colleagues may deteriorate. Your unconscious mind is doing its best to give you what you asked for.

Now, at this stage, you may be wondering or even having negative thoughts and thinking well: "I'm not quite sure I agree with this. I don't believe that thinking can affect the outcome". We will explore the science behind this later. We will discover not only how your thinking affects you, but others around you.

In this book, we're going to focus less on naming the psychological principles, many of which are firmly embedded in academia, and focus more on things that work. When we're buying a car, we don't want to lift the bonnet or the hood and understand what all the wiring around the engine does. We just want to know if we put our foot on the accelerator, or gas pedal, that the car will go and that it will be reliable and not break down.

Some people reading this book will still want some tips. Therefore we will cover some things that you could do consciously to affect your thinking. However, the real secret lies in hacking into your mind, changing your belief systems, sharpening your awareness skills, and learning to manage your state.

There is a lot to cover so let's get started.

CHAPTER 5

The Command Centre

We have learned how our nervous system works. Let's now look at how our brains and minds work. The brain acts as a predictive mechanism. It constantly analyses the environment. It compares the environment that we find ourselves in, against what it predicts that the environment should be like. If the environment is not as predicted, then this is raised to consciousness and processed. Think about walking down the street in your everyday life. You won't remember most of the people that you encounter, except the very attractive person, the unusual looking person, or someone displaying unusual behaviour. This is because unless something is unusual, then this is in line with what the brain expects to experience. There is no point wasting energy in thought analysis needlessly.

Let's look at an example. Suppose that you suddenly see somebody walking towards you wearing a gorilla outfit. This would be classed as unusual. It would not be as predicted and would be raised to consciousness. The same thing occurs if you see an attractive person, a person who looks unusual, or someone who is behaving oddly. Seeing something unusual can snap you out of negative thinking as your attention is diverted, and the brain attempts to make sense of it. This principle is worth remembering.

THE THREE BRAIN BASICS

We have three "brains," with each performing specialised functions (Fig.5). This three-brain model became known as the "triune model" from the work of Paul MacLean. While there have been further refinements, it serves as a good metaphor.

The three brains are:

1. Reptilian, stem brain or paleocortex.
2. Mammalian, midbrain, or limbic system (chimp brain).
3. Human or neocortex brain.

Understanding the Triune

The reptilian brain or paleocortex filters all the incoming messages and handles most of the fight, flight or freeze responses. It is also responsible for some of the very basic and strong primitive emotions. Its prime responsibility is not with thinking, but with survival. When driving a car, if somebody suddenly jumps out in front of the car, we don't want to think about applying the brakes. It's done automatically for us by the reptilian brain, and with it comes the outer expressions.

The midbrain, also known as the mammalian brain or the limbic system, is sometimes referred to as the chimp brain. It makes sense of social situations, attaches meaning to situations and is the emotional centre. The midbrain or chimp brain is the honest part of the brain.

The neocortex is the outer part of the brain responsible for critical thinking and logic. It is responsible for analysing. It will critique and analyse a proposition or proposal. It is our lying brain and will add justification to our behaviour however irrational. The information has to pass through the reptilian brain, to the midbrain and onto the neocortex to be analysed and critiqued. Let's use an example of how the three brains might work.

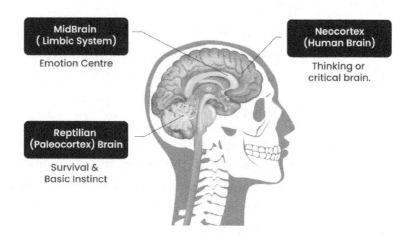

Fig.5

Imagine that you are invited into someone's house and they just mention that they have finished decorating their living room, and it is a shocking, inappropriate colour, and not to your taste. The reptilian brain immediately processes this unexpected and unpredicted change as a mild shock. The limbic brain then puts context into this shocking experience and creates an emotion. This may be disbelief, shock, horror or even humour. The neocortex then analyses the information, and the inner voice may say, "What on earth were they thinking?"

The neocortex attempts to protect us and the other person, as harsh truths can offend. It may cause us to lie to avoid offending and thereby protecting the other person's feelings. The neocortex has worked out that lying is beneficial to us. We may say:

"I love the colour. It really suits you!"

However, this may not be what we are thinking? In business, we may say to our boss:

"I really like the new sales strategy for our company. It sounds very exciting."

However, do we mean it? If we are saying this to others, would it be fair to assume that we may be lying to ourselves also at times? The neocortex is thus the lying brain. It justifies our behaviour. For example,

"It doesn't matter if I steal from them, as they have plenty of money, anyway."

"There is no point in applying for this job. I will never get it, anyway."

Remember, for something to be interpreted as true, it does not have to be true, just plausible. This is very important.

Each of us has our version of reality. We construct this by our brains filtering the data coming in through the primary senses. All this data is generalised, distorted, and deleted and we form our reality from this. We never actually experience full reality, just our version of it. This is our map of the world. This explains why we all like different music, food and holidays, or vacations.

TWIN MIND MASTERY

Let's explore how our mind works, or more specifically, how our twin minds work. We don't have to be mind experts, we just need a basic understanding which will assist us when analysing our negative thoughts. Think about driving a car. We don't have to understand what all the wiring and mechanical components do, but we need to understand what the controls do.

Our minds have two components. We have the conscious mind, which is our critical mind. This can only hold limited pieces of information in our conscious awareness at any point in time. We also have the unconscious mind, which controls activities that are beneath our level of conscious awareness. Let's explore these now.

The Conscious Mind

George Miller, a cognitive psychologist, published a paper in 1956. It is often referred to and used to argue the case that the human mind can hold 7 plus or minus 2 pieces of information in conscious awareness. The 7 plus or minus 2 model serves as a suitable metaphor, but it is more complicated than this. The brain organises information in chunks. Think about your telephone number. How do you remember it? If someone asks for our telephone number, we have a pattern and grouping of numbers that we use to remember this.

Let's suppose your telephone number is 0141 234 5678. The grouping of numbers here is 4 3 4. Now try relaying your number in a different grouping of numbers and notice how difficult it is.

If repeated back in a different grouping of numbers, it can sometimes be confusing. This shows how the brain organises information into groups or chunks. We have a limit to how much information we can process consciously before getting confused. Hypnotists, magicians and pickpockets are aware of this, and use this to their advantage to confuse us.

The conscious mind, therefore, has a very limited bandwidth of data that is brought to consciousness. We do, however, have control over the conscious mind, and we can choose what we want to be consciously aware of. We can move our consciousness and awareness around. For example, you are now aware of the feelings in your left foot, and you can now feel the clothing against your skin. You are now aware of the temperature in the room. There are millions of bits of data coming in, and yet we are not aware of most of them. We can change what we are aware of and think about. This is important when we look at negative thinking.

Our conscious mind is the least well informed and the last to know. It is our lying brain. It lies frequently and often. It justifies our behaviours and the behaviour of others based on our own set of values and beliefs. If the new information or a suggestion fits in with our beliefs and values, then it is accepted. If it doesn't, then our conscious critical mind rejects it. The conscious mind is the critical part of the brain and evaluates information and solves puzzles. It is our higher thinking brain and protects us by analysing information that we have come across previously, and then puts context around it.

While the lower parts of the brain are operating by instinct, the higher part of the brain critically analyses suggestions and statements made. For example, imagine that I told you that a room had a special protective purple light, and that you could put your hand into the fire and not be burned. Your conscious, critical mind would hopefully think that this is highly unlikely.

I would hope that you would seek more information and some proof before engaging in this activity.

Now you may think that is an extreme example. However, you would be surprised at some of the suggestions that have been given over the years and accepted as true because the critical mind has been bypassed. When looking at the suppression of the critical mind, we are moving into the world of hypnosis. This is a big topic and beyond the scope of this book.

The Unconscious Mind

The unconscious mind controls the vast majority of the processes and behaviours that we have. These go on at an unconscious level. It is the engine room, and it controls our breathing, heart rate, blood sugar level, body temperature, together with the digestion and the healing process. There are only two processes that operate unconsciously that we can override consciously, and then only to a limited extent. That is our blinking and our breathing.

The unconscious mind processes around forty million bits of data per second. That is a big difference compared to the conscious mind, which processes around fifty bits of data per second. The unconscious mind, therefore, is a million times more powerful, according to biologist Dr Bruce Lipton.

The unconscious mind always answers first and answers honestly, through emotion, nonverbal signals, and intuition. This is the principle behind Body Language which is covered in detail in the author's book "Body Language How to Read Any Body". There are special ways to communicate with the unconscious mind. The unconscious mind does not critique or analyse, but takes things literally. Its job is to keep us safe and regulate our bodily functions. It responds to imagery, repetition, emotion and stories.

We can think of the unconscious mind a bit like a junction box. We have millions and millions of bits of data coming in via our senses, and yet we are only aware of a tiny amount of it in our conscious awareness. Much of this processing takes place by the unconscious mind. We can decide which switches we want to be turned on at any point in time. Let's switch one on. You are now aware of the sensation in your mouth.

Who's Driving the Bus?

Think of the conscious mind as the driver of the bus. The driver decides how fast to drive the bus, decides when it's going to stop and in what direction to point the bus. Think of the unconscious mind as the bus. It is the engine and all the hardware that makes sure that the bus keeps moving in the direction that the driver points the bus in.

The conscious mind can override our behaviour to a certain extent. However, it takes a lot of effort. Consider if you are out on a date for dinner. Most of us want to give the best possible impression. We make sure when eating that we don't exhibit any bad habits or poor etiquette. We make sure not to speak with our mouths full. Our conscious mind is overriding our natural behaviours, and this takes effort. However, as we become more familiar with somebody, we have less conscious control over our natural patterns of behaviour. The conscious mind thinks about other things, and our etiquette may slip. This may be the same with your negative thinking patterns.

Faulty Bus

Let's return to the bus and suppose that the bus has a fault with it, and it is veering off to the left-hand side. This could represent the challenge that we have with negative thinking. If the bus is constantly veering off to the left-hand side, then the driver has to constantly correct the bus to make sure that it continues to travel in a straight line. If the driver forgets to do this and is not paying attention, then the bus will veer off to the left-hand side and ultimately crash. We need to get into the control area of the bus to correct the fault that is causing it to veer to the left-hand side.

Imagine that all the controls, dials and switches that we need to change and fiddle with are inside a large room, and operate the bus remotely. Now, ideally, we would just like to walk into this control room and make the adjustments. However, there's a problem. For security, a guard has been placed at the entrance.

This engine room represents your unconscious mind, and the guard represents your conscious or critical mind. If we go to the guard, and explain that we want to go into the engine room, and if we can't persuade him or he does not believe this to be in the best interest of the bus, then he won't let us in. Equally, if we can't get into the room to adjust the controls, then the bus is going to carry on veering to the left-hand side. If we want to get past the guard, we have to make sure that his awareness has been suppressed. We can do this in several ways.

We can either, distract the guard so that he is not paying attention, and then sneak in through the door. Alternatively, we can wait until the guard is asleep and then go in and start altering the switches, dials, and settings. Once we are inside the control room with all the levers and dials, we can make minor changes that are needed, and do so without the guard spotting them when he does his security walk. This means that we have to visit this room regularly to make small, subtle changes so that he won't spot them.

This is exactly what the accompanying audio does, which is to get past the guard and make changes without your conscious mind knowing. The audio needs to be used frequently for maximum effect. You can download your audio here. http://www.eliminatenegativethinking.com

Sweet Dreams

The brain cannot tell the difference between something vividly imagined and something experienced. It's the same parts of the brain that light up when measured using fMRI scanning. To illustrate this, let's draw on some of the research.

A group of volunteers were divided into two groups. The first group was asked to play a simple sequence of piano notes each day for five consecutive days. Their brains were scanned each day in the region connected to the finger muscles. The second group was asked to imagine playing the notes instead, and also had their brains scanned each day.

The changes in the brain in those who imagined playing the piano were the same as in those who actually played the piano. This proves that our brain doesn't distinguish real from imaginary! It explains why we can feel nervous or stressed without doing anything. The brain imagines a reality that doesn't exist.

Getting Nervous

The stress response has developed in humans to give us the ability to fight, flight, or flee when faced with danger. While this is very useful, if we are being chased by a dangerous wild animal, it's not particularly useful when talking to ourselves or having negative thoughts. The response will depend on the degree of absorption and vividness of someone's imagination. Sometimes, this can elicit some extreme responses which we explored earlier.

Einstein & Imagination

Einstein knew all about the importance of imagination. Imagination is powerful and nothing in this world would exist if someone had not imagined it at some point. If we think about a bridge, for it to exist, somebody at some point had to imagine it first.

The Other You

If you play golf, drive a car, ride a bicycle, ski or play a musical instrument competently, then who is controlling this? You may think that is a bizarre question and answer it with: "Well, it's me, of course". However, which "me" is it? There is the "you" that you are aware of, but there is also the other "you" that you are not aware of. The unconscious mind is the part that you are unaware of and it controls over ninety five per cent of what we do daily. We could think of this as an iceberg where most of it is hidden from view. This other you controls your thoughts and communication. This is done automatically. It is often when starting to over analyse thoughts that things go wrong.

This conscious mind interference can often cause problems. When you hear of artists, musicians or sports people "being in the zone", they are performing at their peak without having to think about it. Let me share with you a short story to illustrate how conscious thought can interfere with unconscious processes.

I injured my knee while skiing years ago. I was skiing down a very steep mountain ski run at Glencoe in Scotland called the "Flypaper". This is a run that you just don't fall on! I'm a competent skier and I was skiing down the run one day when suddenly, I had a thought. I began to wonder what I was doing to turn the skis as I was doing this unconsciously. In that split moment, I lost control and ended up tumbling to the bottom. This was an incredibly frightening experience, as there was no way to stop. This momentary intervention from my conscious mind resulted in a snapped cruciate ligament.

If you play golf, you will be well aware of the battle that goes on between your mind, and the little voice.

If you're still not convinced that there is another you, why do you refer to the other you? You may have heard people say: "*I'm really annoyed at myself*". Think about that. What does that mean? Who is annoyed and with whom?

Often, experts and sports people perform so much unconsciously that it's quite difficult for them to coach. This is because they don't know what they do. They do it automatically. We see this with musicians too.

Learning to Learn

Think about a time when you learned a new skill. It may have been learning to play a musical instrument, learning to play golf, ski or drive. You may even have tried to learn a foreign language. The learning phase can be quite frustrating. Which part of you is doing this? Well, it's the part that you are aware of, the conscious mind, and it doesn't seem to do it very well.

I enjoy playing the electric guitar and when trying to learn a new solo, it can be incredibly frustrating as my fingers won't go where I want them to. However, I have found that practising in small periods and then having a break seems to help speed up the learning. If I leave it a few days and then return, it seems to be easier. It's almost as if the brain is wiring up while I'm sleeping or away from the musical instrument.

When learning something new, the conscious mind is doing this, and it is the part that we are aware of. Let's look now at how we learn, and how the skills that you will learn from this book will become automatic if you follow the process.

The Four Stages of Learning

When learning a new skill, we go through four stages of learning and these are listed below.

1. Unconscious Incompetence. We are unaware that we don't know how to do something.

2. Conscious Incompetence. We are aware that we don't know how to do something.

3. Conscious Competence. We can now do something but must concentrate, and it is not yet natural.

4. Unconscious Competence. The skill is now hard-wired and we can do it without thinking.

Learning from Chicken Sexers

Separating the egg producing female from male chicks has important commercial value and is a skill called "sexing". The best chicken sexers come from Japan. Separating males from females is difficult, as both look identical to the untrained eye. The training method involves training the brain through trial and error until it becomes an unconscious process. Something that can seem impossible, to begin with soon becomes an unconscious, competent process.

When learning a new skill, it is important to realise the four stages of learning. When going through this book, there may be things you do, are aware of and do well, and there will be things you are less aware of. The key is to break things down and practice them. Trying to learn everything all at once can cause a feeling of being overwhelmed.

Sometimes we can go straight from unconscious incompetence to unconscious competence. If you think about putting your hand in a fire for the first time, you realise that it burns you. This is "one stage learning" and you don't have to keep repeating the activity to know that this is a painful and dangerous thing to do.

The more we practise things then the more they will go from conscious competence to unconscious competence. The best way to learn things is to break them down into small bite-sized chunks.

Eating the Toblerone

A Toblerone chocolate, or candy bar, if you're not familiar with it, is a triangular chocolate bar. It consists of triangular pieces of very hard chocolate connected to make a long triangular shape. The chocolate is very hard because of its triangular shape and pointy edges.

If I was to give you a Toblerone chocolate or candy bar and ask you to put it in your mouth and bite into it, it would be painful to bite. However, if we break the Toblerone down into small triangular chunks and eat one piece at a time, then it becomes much easier.

Using the Toblerone analogy, the more that we can break things down into simple pieces then the easier it is for us to learn. As we learn, those pieces become gelled together just like the Toblerone bar, until eventually we have mastered the skill and have a full Toblerone.

CHAPTER 6

The Power of Belief

O f all the factors affecting negative thinking, the power
of belief is the greatest contributor. Many of our
fundamental beliefs are laid down early in life. These
beliefs come from our parents, schools and our life experiences.
Such is the power of belief that it can radically change what you
believe is possible. I picked up a belief when I was a child that I
am not very good at art. This came from a lesson at school in
which we had to slice a tomato in half and paint it. My attempt
wasn't the best, and the teacher laughed at it. That was the last
painting that I did.

We're going to delve deep into the power of belief. If you are
reading this book, you may have tried lots of tips before, and
found them not to work. This is because it is not the conscious
you that is controlling your behaviours and thoughts. It is the
other you.

People must change their own beliefs but can be assisted on
the journey. If you engage in negative thinking, it can be very
annoying when someone says: "Just look on the bright side!"
While these comments can be well meant, we may think to

ourselves: "Don't you think that I've not thought about that before"! It's a bit like saying to someone who is a drug addict: "Just say no".

Resistance

People tend to resist what they are told and accept what they conclude. Therefore, if I was to give you a tip and say: "You need to change your belief system and change your life", there may be several reactions.

1. You may have the internal voice saying "F you!" Don't tell me I need to do anything!
2. You may be curious and wonder how belief systems are changed.
3. You may need to be convinced by the power of belief.
4. You may not believe me and want some supporting evidence.
5. You may feel that negative thinking is something that you were born with and that there is nothing you can do about it.

Rather than trying to force you into a particular way of thinking, in this chapter, we're going to be looking at the evidence for the effect of belief on the outcome, and how beliefs are established in the first place. There is a lot of material to get through. If possible, try to suspend disbelief and just go with the flow. You can then make your mind up, and either accept it or reject it.

We discovered in the previous chapter how reality is an illusion and is subjective to each one of us. Let's look at how beliefs are set up.

The Origin of Beliefs

Beliefs are set up by filtering external data through a series of psychological filters. Beliefs are given to us at an early age by our parents and then through education and institutions by authority figures. There are individual beliefs that are specific to each individual, but there are also cultural beliefs. Cultural beliefs, or cultural trances, are very often not questioned, and result in group thinking or cultural trance, where people behave without critiquing the information. This can result in not only self-imposed limitations but also self-limiting beliefs imposed upon us from group thinking. Most of this takes place between the ages of two to twelve years old when the brain is predominantly in the Alpha-Theta state. This is a more suggestible and programmable state. The brain waves in this state correspond to a deep relaxation that many people will go into during meditation or hypnosis. We are not trapped in a cycle of negative thinking because of our past events, but because of our inability to engage in change.

Cultural Trances

A good example of a cultural trance was recorded over four hundred years ago when Magellan was circumnavigating the earth and stopped at Terra del Fuego. The Fuegians were a canoe based culture, and as they had never seen tall ships before, they could not comprehend this, and to them, they did not exist. The brain filtered out the data based on expectation and provided a negative hallucination, which is a hypnotic phenomenon. As Magellan and his crewmates rowed ashore, the Fuegians were puzzled as to where they had come from. Magellan pointed to the tall ships, yet the Fuegians could not see them and assumed that Magellan and his crew were gods that had come down from the sky. In frustration, Magellan rowed the natives out to show them the ships. As they came closer the ships came into view for them. Initially, as the natives had never experienced the ships before, they simply filtered out this information. This has been recorded in Magellan's diaries and makes fascinating reading. Similar instances have been recorded by Columbus too when he arrived in Santa Domingo. His ships looked like shimmering heat waves devoid of definition to the natives.

A more recent example is when American soldiers, after having set up a base in Greenland, took Polaroid pictures of the Eskimos to help build rapport. The Eskimos couldn't see any definition in the Polaroid pictures as they did not expect to see an image there.

Some of you may be thinking that this is farfetched or hard to believe. However, have you ever looked for your car keys, or perhaps you've been looking in the refrigerator, or for something or in a cupboard, and you just can't see the item you're looking for? Then the moment it is pointed out by somebody else it comes into view. This is an example of a negative hallucination, and it's indicative of a deep hypnotic trance.

If the brain can create negative hallucinations as shown with the Fuegian natives and the Eskimos in the above examples, what else might the brain be hallucinating about? Could negative thinking be one of them?

The psychologist David Phillips wanted to investigate whether the beliefs of people can influence life expectancy. He looked at the mortality data for Jewish and Chinese people around major significant cultural events and festivals. He found that there was a statistically significant drop in mortality around this time compared with the previous six months. There was also an increase in mortality for the six months after the significant events. This would seem to imply that people can "will" themselves to live longer to participate in the significant event.

Getting People Out of Trance

I heard a very profound statement from a hypnotist who said: "The issue is not getting people into a trance but getting them out of the one that they are already in!" This is not a book on hypnosis. However, hypnosis does give an insight into how the unconscious mind works. There are many definitions for hypnosis. My definition is "a suppression of critical thinking so that suggestions are accepted and acted upon, together with an absorption in the experience". When beliefs are accepted without any critical thought, whether on an individual basis or as part of group think, then this can be described as a type of trance.

Think about when you drive your car, and a few miles or kilometres may have gone by, and you have no recollection of part of the drive. This is a form of hypnosis. It has been estimated that we repeat over eighty per cent of our activities daily. Many of these are done unconsciously, without us being aware of what we're doing.

When it comes to thought patterns, it has been estimated that we have over ninety per cent of recurring thoughts every day. How much of your thinking is done unconsciously, and results in negative thoughts?

As we go through the book, we will look at how we can come out of the trance, and self imposed negative thinking that we put ourselves in. We are all prisoners of our perceptions and beliefs that have been programmed into us by our culture, teachers, books, the media and authority figures.

The Belief Hard Drive

Let's consider where our beliefs are stored and we will use a computer as an analogy. Beliefs are stored and accessed by our unconscious mind, which is the equivalent of the hard drive of the computer. It makes sure that our external reality ties into our belief system.

Let's use an example and suppose that our belief system is that we can't close any deals. Your unconscious mind helps to make this a reality for you. If it detects that you are about to close a deal, then it wants to maintain this belief system for you. If you believe that you are unable to close any deals, you may find yourself saying, or doing, self sabotaging things to ensure that you fail. The unconscious mind takes things literally and does its best to help you reinforce your current beliefs. As Henry Ford said:

"Whether you think you can, or think you can't, you are right."

Let's now explore some of the science behind "belief" to show how our thoughts can affect the outcome. For this, we're going to move into the world of medicine.

In the next chapter, we will explore the fascinating subject of placebos.

CHAPTER 7

Belief for Good & Bad

PLACEBOS

Howard Fields, at the University of California, defines a placebo as something that provides an improvement in a condition, attributable to an expectation of benefit. The word placebo comes from Latin and means, "I will please". Placebos range in effectiveness from thirty one per cent to seventy two per cent in pain management studies.

One of the earliest examples of placebos was documented over three hundred and fifty years ago by Charles II the English King, who is said to have cured a hundred thousand people during his reign simply by laying his hands on them.

Placebos often can masquerade as drugs, and look like drugs, but are often no more than sugar pills. Research has been carried out with patients who experienced migraines. Researchers asked all of their subjects to refrain from taking any medication for two hours after the onset of their first migraine. The subjects were then given six envelopes, each containing a pill to be taken during their next six migraine attacks. Two of the envelopes were labelled "Maxalt", a drug used for the treatment of migraines. Two of the envelopes indicated that the pill inside could either be "Maxalt" or the placebo". The final two envelopes were labelled "Placebo". Subjects then rated the amount of pain two hours after taking each pill. When subjects took no pills, they reported a fifteen per cent increase in migraine pain after two hours. When they took a pill labelled placebo, they reported a twenty six per cent reduction in pain. When they took a pill labelled as Maxalt, they reported a forty per cent reduction in pain.

However, when they took a pill that could have been either a placebo or Maxalt, they also reported a forty per cent decrease in pain. Incredibly, the placebo labelled as Maxalt was equally effective as the actual Maxalt drug.

Surely This Would Never Work?

Surgeon J. Bruce Mosely of Baylor College of Medicine, Houston, Texas, has carried out numerous operations for osteoarthritis of the knee over the years. He shook the medical establishment with his discovery. Crippling pain from osteoarthritis is a loss of essential joint cartilage and can be very painful and debilitating for the person suffering from it. This has been treated with surgery in which a tiny camera is inserted into the knee and guides the surgery. First, the surgeon checks for any tears in the cartilage. There is then a two-step process. Debris is removed from the knee joint and any rough cartilage is smoothed down. Dr Moseley wondered which part of the surgery was the most effective, the first part or the second.

An experiment was devised to test one form of surgery against the other. When Dr Mosely consulted a colleague, Nelda Wray, also of the Baylor College of Medicine, Houston, Texas,

70

she pointed out that they would have to set up a control placebo surgery as well. When Dr Moseley first heard about this, he almost laughed out loud because at the time everyone knew there was no such thing as placebo surgery.

His colleagues randomly placed one hundred and eighty osteoarthritis patients into three treatment groups. The first group had surgery in which loose or worn cartilage was cut away. The second group had surgery in which the bad cartilage was flushed out with liquid. The third group had sham surgery. The surgery was carried out as if it was real surgery with an incision made.

Two army veterans, Tim Perez, a corporal in the Korean War, and Sylvester Colligan, a corporal in World War 2, were amongst the first placebo surgery patients. Dr Mosely made three incision cuts in the knee and pretended to carry out the sham surgery. To add authenticity, he would ask for the various instruments as if carrying out a real operation. Doctor Moseley wanted to make this appear as real as possible and had a video of a real surgery playing in the background, to help re-enact the surgical procedure accurately. After thirty minutes, he stitched up the three incisions after having done absolutely nothing to the knee.

The results were amazing and were identical in all three groups. Bruce Moseley commented that his skills as a surgeon had no impact on the outcome of the operation. It was found that the entire benefit of arthroscopic surgery of the knee was due to the placebo effect. In other words, it wasn't the washing and rinsing and suturing of the knee that caused the improvement, but the ritual surrounding the surgery.

This was not just a temporary fix. Six years after the surgery, Sylvester Corrigan could walk again normally and his knee didn't bother him at all. Before receiving the sham surgery, he was in severe pain and was struggling to walk. Another patient, Tim Perez, responded so well to the sham surgery that he could now play basketball again with his grandchildren, after previously requiring a stick to walk.

A One Off?

David Kallmes from the Mayo Clinic has been repairing broken backs using a type of cement that is injected into the bone known as vertebroplasty. He decided to put his surgery to the test. He wanted to test this with placebo surgery. He was called a heretic for even suggesting to try this. He carried out the sham surgery and made sure to mimic all parts of the procedure accurately. Bonnie Anderson was part of the trial and previously was in severe pain and unable to do any housework. Within a week of the operation, she was able to play golf again. There was no statistical difference in pain relief or functioning between patients who had the actual surgery and those who had the sham surgery.

Bone Removal

Professor Andy Carr of Oxford University in 2012 conducted acromioplasty. The operation involves removing a spur of bone from the shoulder which is thought to remove pain but had never been tested. Volunteers were randomly selected with some receiving the real surgery and others the sham surgery. For the sham surgery, the patients would be cut open but the bone would be left intact. Carol Brennan was one such patient in the sham surgery group who made a miraculous recovery and with it full mobility. When the results were analysed, again there was no difference between the sham surgery and the actual surgery.

Depressed Results

Research from scanning patients' brains with depression who have responded to placebos found there is an increase in activity at the front of the brain associated with mood. Concerning placebos, Dr Andrew Leuchter surmised: "It's not just in your head it's a real physical process that changes the function of the brain".

Pain Relief Placebo

Irving Kirsch, professor of psychology at the University of Connecticut, under a Freedom of Information Request in 2001, received drug company data submitted by top drug companies to support the licencing of six top anti-depressants.

The difference in the response to the drug versus the placebo was less than two points on a clinical scale of fifty to sixty points. This difference is meaningless. In 2003, he hit the headlines where it was claimed that anti-depressants didn't work. However, people missed the point. It is the belief in the drug or placebo that is causing the effect. For the pharmaceutical industry to publish this data would mean that it could negatively impact on the efficacy of the drugs. As there has been a tightening in the use of placebos, the healthcare industry is caught between a rock and a hard place. What can they do? If it is the belief that is creating the healing then the belief in the pharmaceutical industry's expertise has an effect.

If your belief is strong enough and you have been conditioned to believe that if somebody hitting you on the head with a pencil would cure your depression, then it is likely to work with at least 30 per cent of people. Protecting that belief is key to its success.

The Effect of Belief on Others

It is well known that a person's belief in the hypnotist affects the ability to be hypnotised. However, hypnotist and mind control researcher, George Estabrooks, established that the belief of the hypnotist affects the ability to hypnotise the subject too.

In medicine, attention is often given to the role that a patient's belief in a particular treatment plays and its efficacy. There is, however, also the question of the Doctor's belief and the effect that it has on the outcome. It has been shown that the Doctor's belief in a particular therapy can, and does affect the outcome for a patient. This has been shown in double-blind experiments.

Double-blind studies have been examined by Jerry Solfvin to examine the effect of using vitamin E in the treatment of pain associated with coronary artery disease. One of the doctors in the study enthusiastically believed in the power of vitamin E, while the other three doctors did not. Surprisingly, the results of the double-blind studies matched the doctor's beliefs. The enthusiastic doctor found the effects of Vitamin E to be better than the placebo, while the other two doctors did not.

Solfvin also cites another case. In the 1950s there were conflicting reports about meprobamate, a tranquillizing drug. A double-blind study was designed. One of the doctors administering the drug felt positive and enthusiastic about it and the other was sceptical about whether it would work. Neither the doctors nor the patients knew whether they were involved with the drug or the placebo, and did not know that they were part of an experiment. The results for the drug proved more effective for the patients of the enthusiastic doctor but were no better than the placebo for the sceptical doctor.

In all these stories and studies, something very important has emerged. The power of belief can, in many cases, override reality. The outcome seems to be affected not just by the recipient's belief, but also by the belief of the operator. This is profound and, in relation to negative thinking, is worth exploring and thinking long and hard about. Argue for your weakness and it's yours!

NOCEBO

The evil twin of the placebo is the nocebo. This is a belief that a drug or a certain action may cause you harm. Doctors themselves are both placebos and nocebos depending on how they communicate the message. Professor Howard Fields MD from the University of California explains that words have power and affect the brain. This can be beneficial or harmful. The power of words is explored in more detail with some fascinating results in Chapter 11. If you communicate to a patient that you don't think that a medication is going to work through your tone of voice or body language, then this affects the efficacy of the medication. Belief in a negative outcome can also affect outcomes, as we shall see next.

Patients at a hospital in Birmingham in the UK with gastric cancer were divided into two groups. The first group received chemotherapy and the second group received the placebo but were told that they were receiving chemotherapy. One third of the patients in the placebo group displayed the side effects of chemotherapy, including hair loss and nausea.

One of the most disturbing cases of the nocebo relates to Sam Londe in 1974. The outcome deeply affected his physician

Clifton Meador from St Thomas Hospital, Nashville. Sam Londe was a retired salesman who had been diagnosed with cancer of the oesophagus. The surgeon had removed the cancer that they found during surgery, but they were convinced that it would return. In 1974 there were no survivors of oesophageal cancer. It was not a surprise to anyone that he died not long after. When a post mortem was conducted there were only two tiny nodes of cancer in his liver and one in his lung. However, they were very small and not enough to kill him. There was no cancer of the oesophagus that everyone assumed had killed him. Sam Londe died *with* cancer and not *of* cancer. Clifton Meador was haunted by the fact that he may have taken away hope from Sam Londe through his words and belief system.

The power of a doctor with a white coat and a stethoscope, placed around the neck, conveys a certain message that we have interpreted over the years. It's hard to accept, but in many cases, according to the research, the very fact that the doctor walks in with a white coat and a stethoscope plays a significant part in the healing process.

Can We Train Belief?

One of the stumbling blocks for possible placebo use is that it is only effective for one in three people. However, a unique experiment carried out by neuroscientist Professor Fabio Benedetti of the University of Turin looked to see if we can train people's belief systems and, with it make a placebo more effective.

A volunteer was selected to receive electric shocks to the forehead. On admission of each electric shock, the volunteer had to rate the pain on a 1-10 scale. After the first shock, the volunteer rated the pain as a 10. The volunteer is then given an injection and told that it is a pain killer. On the subsequent shock, he rates the pain as a 7. He thinks that the anaesthetic has caused a reduction in pain. However, Benedetti lied to him and he was actually given a saline solution injection as a placebo. The reason he feels less pain is because the amount of shock he received was lower. This is repeated for a second time. The volunteer is shocked, given a fake pain killer and then shocked again with a less intensive shock. The third time the volunteer is shocked and then given a fake pain killer. However this time the intensity of the shock has not been reduced. Remarkably the volunteer feels less pain. His brain has been conditioned to experience less pain. By conditioning patients, Professor Benedetti has managed to boost placebo response rates from thirty to ninety per cent.

Reality really can be manipulated and experienced differently. This has profound effects for negative thinking. If we can train ourselves to believe that a placebo can be effective. Do you think it is possible to train ourselves out of negative thinking? I believe so.

Belief Putting Cancer in Remission

One of the most extraordinary stories about the power of belief relates to an article in 1957 in the Journal of Projective Techniques referencing the physician Philip West and his patient, Mr Wright. The story is so extraordinary that had it not been documented in the official Medical Journal, it could have been thought of as pure fantasy.

Mr Wright had an advanced malignancy associated with the lymph nodes known as lymphosarcoma. Mr Wright was under the care of Dr Philip West and was in a terminal state requiring an oxygen mask to assist with his breathing. He had large tumours the size of oranges in his neck, groin, chest, and abdomen. He had between one to two litres (33-68 oz.) of milky fluid drawn from his chest every other day.

However, Mr Wright was not without hope. A new drug was being developed called Krebiozen and Philip West's clinic had been chosen by the Medical Association for the evaluation of the treatment. Mr Wright was considered ineligible for the trial because of his short life expectancy of only a few weeks.

When the drug arrived, Wright pleaded with Philip West to be included in the trial. West gave in and agreed to allow Wright to be part of the test. On Friday morning before the treatment, Wright was gasping for air and completely bedridden. The drug was then administered intravenously, and Philip West did not see him again until Monday morning.

Upon returning, West was astonished to see Wright up and about and chatting to the nurses without his oxygen mask. Wright's progress had been amazing, and in a matter of days, the tumours had shrunk like snowballs on a hot stove to half of their original size. Observing this, Philip West was eager to check on the other patients who had received the same injection. The other patients showed no change, if anything, they were worse.

The injections continued three times a day and within ten days, Mr Wright was discharged from his deathbed, with practically all signs of the disease having been banished. He was now breathing normally and could fly his plane at 12000 feet (3657 metres) with no discomfort.

After two months, reports started coming out from all the testing clinics that Krebiozen was not effective and that there were no positive results so far. This troubled Wright, and he began to lose faith. After two months of perfect health, he relapsed into his original state.

At this point, Philip West thought there was an opportunity to double-check the drug, and took advantage of Wright's optimism to conduct a scientific experiment. West decided to lie to Mr Wright and say that he was not to believe what he was reading in the newspapers, and that initial results with the drug had been very promising. He told him that the next day a new version of the drug was arriving, which was a super strength drug.

Philip West waited a few days before administering the drug intravenously in an identical manner. On this occasion, Wright's recovery was even more dramatic. The tumours melted, the chest fluid vanished, and he went back to flying his plane again. However, these injections that Phillip West was administering were not a super strength version of Krebiozen but freshwater!

The final AMA announcement then appeared in the press, stating that Krebiozen was a worthless drug in the treatment of cancer. Within a few days of this report, Mr Wright was re-admitted to the hospital, his faith now gone, and he died in less than two days.

Belief Overriding Genetics

Albert Mason was a young anaesthesiologist who often used hypnotism to treat pain and cure common ailments. This amazing story is documented in the British Medical Journal. The case in 1951 concerns a young boy aged 16 whose skin was covered in black warts except for his chest, neck, and face. The skin was as hard as a fingernail and would crack on the surface and leak blood stained serum.

In an attempt to help the patient, the boy underwent skin graft surgery. Unfortunately, the two skin grafts were unsuccessful. Mason suggested to one of the surgeons to try hypnosis, as it had been reported as being very successful in curing warts. The surgeon, not amused, said: "Well, why don't you try it!"

Treatment by hypnosis began on the 10th of February, 1951. The patient was hypnotised and under hypnosis, a suggestion was made that the left arm would clear. After about five days, the hard layer of skin softened and fell off. Within a few days, the skin became pink and soft. At the end of ten days, the arm was completely clear from shoulder to wrist.

What is remarkable about this story is that the boy didn't have a bad case of warts, but had "congenital ichthyosiform erythroderma", or Brocq's disease, for which there is no cure. Once Mason discovered that there had been a misdiagnosis and that it was not a case of warts, he was unable to repeat the treatment. His belief had changed.

Suggestion & Medical Students

Research shows that when medical students are learning about a disease, about seventy to eighty per cent will experience the actual symptoms of whatever disease they are learning about at the time. It is even more surprising because even if they are warned by their lecturer to anticipate this phenomenon; it makes little difference. The students continue to perceive the symptoms as real. As the students learn about different diseases, it has been referred to as the "disease of the week".

This has long been known by medical professionals and as far back as 1908, the physician George Lincoln Walton wrote: "Medical instructors are continually consulted by students who fear that they have the diseases they are studying. The knowledge that pneumonia produces pain in a certain spot leads to a concentration of attention upon that region, which causes any sensation there to raise an alarm. The mere knowledge of the location of the appendix transforms the most harmless sensations in that region into symptoms of serious menace."

BELIEF FOR PERFORMANCE

In an experiment, Dr Chris Beedie from Aberystwyth University assembled a group of some of the UK's top cyclists at the Manchester velodrome. He wanted to see if he could make the cyclists cycle faster than ever before. The riders first rode as fast as they could to establish a baseline speed. Then, four hours later, they were told that they would be given legal performance enhancing supplements for their second test run. Half of the riders were to be given caffeine supplements and the other half were told they were to be given a supplement containing caffeine, nitrate and bicarbonate. Both capsules were the same, and both were filled with cornflour. This was not disclosed to the cyclists who believed they were taking part in an experiment to see if the placebo could improve performance. Astonishingly, more than half were quicker with the cornflour. One cyclist even set a personal best, being two tenths of a second quicker.

PLACEBO REAL OR IMAGINED

At a mountain top location in Italy where the air is thinner, Professor Fabrizio Benedetti conducted an experiment to test the effects of oxygen on someone who expected to receive oxygen. A volunteer was selected and was told that an experiment was taking place to show the effects of increased oxygen on performance. The volunteer was asked to set off on a hike in the mountains and given a face mask connected to what he was told was an oxygen supply in a backpack. The backpack did not contain any additional oxygen. When the volunteer set off, the researchers very soon had difficulty keeping up with him. The question was, had the fake oxygen just given a psychological boost or had it changed something in his body?

When at high altitude, the low oxygen level in our blood causes the neurotransmitter PGE2 to rise. This can give the symptoms of altitude sickness. However, by giving extra oxygen, the PGE2 level falls again. This means feeling less pain and it is easier to carry out activities. Remarkably when the fake oxygen is given to the volunteer and levels of PGE2 are measured, it was found that the PGE2 levels fall while blood oxygen saturation levels remain constant. This shows that it is the expectation of the placebo that is causing the physiological changes. This caused less feelings of pain and so enabled them to hike faster. Belief has altered physiology.

EVEN WHEN FAKE

A Seaside Town

In a BBC television programme entitled "Can my brain cure my body?", Dr Michael Mosley set up an experiment to see if back pain could be relieved using no more than a placebo.

In the seaside town of Blackpool in the UK, one in five people suffer from back pain. One hundred and seventeen people were invited to take part in an experiment. Many of the volunteers had been experiencing back pain for years. To make the experiment as real as possible, a GP (Doctor's) surgery was chosen on the outskirts of the town to be used as a medical centre for authenticity. On entering the surgery there was a sign saying *"Opticare, Optimising Back Pain Care"*, together with a logo to enhance authenticity. When the volunteers arrived at the medical centre, they had a brief wait before seeing the doctor as this is normal. Volunteers were then met by one of four doctors and given pain relief capsules. Blue and white capsules were to be taken twice a day. Research shows that the colour of the capsule affects the outcome. Blue and white capsules have an analgesic effect as opposed to red and white, which have been shown to have a stimulation effect.

Patients were then asked to fill in a disability score question sheet before the treatment and then on completion of the treatment. The container containing the capsules had warnings displayed on it, very similar to conventional pharmaceutical medicines. To make it even more authentic, the volunteers were told they may receive the real painkiller or a placebo. As part of the experiment, the researchers were also testing whether having more time with the doctor would boost the efficacy of the pain relief pills. In one group, the patients received the standard consulting time with the doctor, which is nine minutes and twenty two seconds while the second group could spend up to thirty minutes with the doctor.

The results of the placebo experiment demonstrated a forty five per cent medical improvement. When the data was further analysed, it was shown that patients who received the standard time with the doctor showed a thirty eight per cent improvement compared with a fifty one per cent to those who received the longer consultation period.

As part of a further experiment, the patients who were given the placebos were told to carry on taking the capsules, knowing that they were no more than a placebo. Surprisingly even when knowing this, seventy per cent of the people felt the beneficial effects of the placebo.

In this section, we have looked at the profound effect that belief can have on medical treatment and the corresponding physiological changes.

What has all this got to do with negative thinking? You may now be contemplating the power of belief. If a belief can affect the outcome, as shown in these studies, is it possible that your negative thinking may come from your beliefs? What effect does belief have on effects other than medical, and is it possible for a belief to change the outcome? Let's explore this further in the next chapter.

CHAPTER 8

Mind Over Matter

We have already seen that taking a placebo can affect the outcome, as shown in many experiments, and the importance belief has on this. We have learned about the power of the mind and its healing and performance enhancing capabilities. However, can thoughts affect events? Perhaps if you're in a pattern of negative thinking you may think that this is not possible. Let's have a look at the scientific research and see if there is any merit in the statement that thoughts can affect the outcome.

We don't want to delve too heavily into the scientific details, however, some experiments are worth considering. These show that the world is perhaps not the way that we think it is, and there are some things that we just cannot explain. This is important to realise as we expand our mind and awareness, which are an important part to eliminate negative thinking. Let's begin.

The Effect of Thoughts

Let's have a look and see if our thoughts can influence the outcome just by consciously thinking about something.

Dr Helmut Schmidt was a former research physicist with Boeing. Schmidt conducted an experiment in which he connected two random event generators, to generate truly random results, to a red light and a green light which created a random flashing of red and green lights. Thirty five subjects were asked to make the red light come on more often than the green light.

The results showed a statistically significant event. Nineteen other scientists have since replicated Schmidt's experiment, including the Sceptic Society! Let's now look at how our minds can affect our bodies.

Drying the Laundry

Doctor Herbert Benson of the Harvard Medical School has investigated the effects of meditation on the body's metabolism. He conducted experiments on Buddhist monks from Tibetan monasteries. He found that oxygen consumption was reduced by upwards of 64 per cent using a simple, restful procedure. When using a type of meditation known as "tummo", the Yogis were able to generate inner heat. Doctor Benson's results found that the monks were able to increase their skin temperature in environments of 50-60 degrees Fahrenheit (10 - 15.5 degrees Celsius). He also discovered that these monks in very cold environments of 40 degrees Fahrenheit (5.5 degrees Celsius) could increase the temperature of their bodies sufficiently to cause wet sheets to steam and to dry.

Most normal people would go into uncontrollable shivering, and perhaps even die from having too low blood pressure. Yet

86

the monks were quite comfortable performing their tummo meditational heat yoga. We now have evidence that our thoughts affect our health, can alter events and can affect our bodies. We have now seen that the mind can affect matter.

Let's explore next if negative thinking is genetic and if we are trapped with this problem due to our genes.

CHAPTER 9

It's Genetic Isn't It?

There is a common misconception that negative thinking and any corresponding anxiety, are completely under the control of our genes. At the time of writing, there is no evidence beyond question that supports a single genetic cause of anxiety or negative thinking. In this section, we will be referencing the excellent work of Bruce H Lipton and his book "The Biology of Belief".

The media frequently displays headlines stating that scientists have discovered a gene for a particular condition. However, upon closer scrutiny, the evidence does not stack up. We will cover this in more detail in this chapter.

In a paper published in Molecular Psychiatry in 2019, it was claimed that chromosome nine carries genes associated with the development of anxiety. However, having these genes does not necessarily mean that you will develop anxiety. We will be exploring this in this chapter together with evidence to support this. We will look at our thoughts and how they affect our genes. While science debates nature versus nurture, it is very difficult to separate a learned behaviour from one of genetic origin. It is the author's opinion that negative thinking and anxiety are not solely of genetic origin, but are a combination of factors.

We must be very careful when associating a genetic component with human behaviour. Human beings look for meaning in everything, and as long as it is plausible, it may be believed, but this does not mean that it is true.

We have seen in previous chapters the power of belief, the power of suggestion, and how this manifests from the belief in placebos and nocebos.

Questioning Genetics

In his book published in 1859 entitled: "The Origin of Species", Darwin concluded that individual traits or hereditary factors are passed from parents to their offspring. Following this publication, scientists began searching for just where these hereditary factors are located.

When James Watson and Francis Crick discovered the structure and function of the DNA double Helix from which genes are made, scientists were convinced that they had discovered the secret to these hereditary factors. This discovery dominated the newspapers and back in 1953 there were headlines of "Secret of Life Discovered".

The mechanism by which DNA controlled biological life became the scientific dogma in the long running debate of nature versus nurture. The discovery resulted in consensus thinking moving towards genetic predisposition. Initially, it was believed that DNA was only responsible for our physical characteristics, but then consensus changed, resulting in the acceptance of genes influencing our emotions and behaviour too. This led to the belief that genes could affect happiness and consequently result in someone being a negative thinker.

Near his death, however, Darwin acknowledged that his evolutionary theory had not given enough importance to the effect of the environment. In 1876 Darwin wrote a letter to Moritz Wagner highlighting:

"In my opinion, the greatest error which I have committed has been not allowing sufficient weight to the direct action of the environments, i.e., food, climate, etc., independently of natural selection … When I wrote the Origin, and for some years afterwards, I could find little good evidence of the direct action of the environment; now there is a large body of evidence." (Darwin, F 1888)

Some diseases like Huntington's chorea, beta thalassemia, and cystic fibrosis are caused by one single faulty gene. However, single gene disorders affect less than two per cent of the population. Most people have all the genes that should enable them to live a healthy and happy life. Today's problem diseases such as diabetes, heart disease, and cancer are not as a result of a single gene but a complex interaction among many genes together with environmental factors.

Headlines often imply that scientists have discovered a gene responsible for a particular element, perhaps depression or anxiety. However, on closer inspection, rarely has this found to have been isolated to one gene being responsible for a particular trait or disease.

The confusion occurs when the media repeatedly confuses the meaning of two words, namely correlation and causation. It's one thing to be linked to a disease. It's another to cause disease. Causing implies a directing, controlling action.

In a paper, Metaphors and the Role of Genes and Development by H. F. Nijhout. (Nijhout 1990), Nijhout presents evidence that the notion that genes control biology has been so frequently repeated for such a long time that scientists have forgotten that it is a hypothesis and not a truth. Nijhout summarises the truth:

> *"When a gene product is needed, a signal from its environment, not an emergent property of the gene itself, activates expression of that gene." - HF Nijhout*

In other words, when it comes to genetic control, it's the environment.

Our cells are made up of four types of very large molecules: polysaccharides (complex sugars), lipids (fats), nucleic acids (DNA/RNA), and proteins. Of these components, proteins are the most important when it comes to living cells. Our trillion cells plus bodies are composed of protein chains. Our bodies can be considered as protein generating machines. We consist of over 100,000 proteins. Scientists have mapped the human genome project to map out all the human genes. They expected to find one gene for one protein.

However, what they actually discovered was that there were only 25,000 genes. This created a problem because 80% of the expected proteins were missing. The concept of one gene for one protein and the ability to genetically engineer, now has major flaws. There are not enough genes to cater to the complexity of human life and the number of diseases.

David Baltimore, one of the world's preeminent geneticists and a Nobel Prize winner, in 2001, addressed the issue of human complexity:

> *"But unless the human genome contains a lot of genes that are opaque to our computers, it is clear that we do not gain our undoubted complexity over worms and plants by using more genes."*

The results of the Human Genome Project have forced us to consider other ideas about how life is controlled. As Baltimore points out:

"Understanding what does give us our complexity... remains a challenge for the future."

Geneticists have discovered that human beings and rodents have roughly the same number of genes. Our genes are located in the nucleus of the cell. Think about drawing a large circle and then within it drawing a smaller circle at the centre. The smallest circle would represent the nucleus. If the genes are the brain or command centre of the cell, then if they are removed, the cell should die. However, it has been found that the cell can still live for two months or more when the nucleus and the genetic material are removed. The nucleus with the genes cannot be the command centre.

The Brain of the Cell

If the nucleus is not the brain of the cell, as previously thought, what is the nucleus, and more importantly, what are our genes for? Genes do not cause anything they are merely potential and need to be activated. The question is, how are they activated? Genes are just blueprints. They are dependent on a signal from the environment to activate the gene and activate the expression of that gene. There are two environments. There is the internal environment which is dependent on the physiology of your body, and there is also the external environment. If the nucleus of the cell is not the command centre, then what is?

The command centre of the cell is the cell membrane. The nucleus of the cell is for reproduction. On the surface of the cell are located two types of proteins. There are receptor proteins and channel proteins. Each receptor protein has an antenna associated with it that responds to different stimuli. Some may respond to glucose, some may respond to insulin, and some respond to photons of light. These receptors are connected to a channel type of tunnel that opens up in response to a signal and allows this signal or molecule to pass through the membrane to inside the cell. This signal affects the activities of the cell. This means that environmental factors affect behaviour. Perception and awareness of the environment are controlled through physical sensation. Therefore, we are controlled by perception. Perception is controlled by the brain by interpreting the environment.

The field of epigenetics, which means control above genetics, has challenged the conventional theory that genes passed down are not set in concrete for the outcome, but are a mere potential.

Environmental influences, including stress, emotions and nutrition, can modify those genes without changing their basic blueprint. These modifications, as epigeneticists have discovered, can be passed on to future generations as DNA blueprints and are passed on via the double helix. For example, stress is a signal perceived by the brain. The same hormones that suppress the immune system during stress are given to patients receiving transplants. This shuts down the immune system to conserve energy. When stress levels get high, often sickness results, and we can't blame our genes. Maintaining chronic stress isn't from our genes, but our beliefs. Stress alters our systems, and the stress signals come to the cell membrane and activate the protein pathways.

Only five per cent of women have hereditary breast cancer. Convention says that gene mutation is random. In an experiment, bacteria that had a defective lactose enzyme were placed in a petri dish. This means that they were unable to break down lactose. A lactose solution was added to the petri dish. Having a defective lactase enzyme means that the bacteria should not be able to use lactose as food, and hence should not be able to divide or mutate.

However, after a few days, there were colonies of bacteria living in the petri dish from cell division. The bacteria had changed their lactase defective gene! Mutations were not random, but the bacteria were adapting to the environment. Your beliefs will rewrite the genes to accommodate your belief, which may be negative thinking.

In this very important chapter, we have discovered that our limitations and negative thinking are not a result of one particular gene. The evidence for this is overwhelming and our genes are only a potential that can be altered by our thoughts. We have seen the effects of the power of thought both in healing and in bringing about an early death. Our destiny is not predetermined but is very much in our own hands, except for less than five per cent of genetically inherited diseases.

We are not slaves to our genes and we can learn to change our thinking and enhance every aspect of our life. I hope that this chapter has been insightful and has explained how important controlling our thoughts is. Let's now explore reality.

CHAPTER 10

Making Sense of It

W
e have discovered that our genes represent a potential and account for less than five per cent of genetic diseases. We have also learned that thoughts can affect the outcome. If our thoughts do indeed affect our reality, then what is reality and how do we create it?

In this chapter, we're going to look at just how we encode our world. It is a fascinating chapter and we will explore our own maps of the world that are unique to us. This is important because once we understand this, then we can start to make changes as we head toward some of the techniques in Part Two of the book.

Inside Out

In this chapter, we are going to draw from information from the author's earlier work, "How to Talk to Anybody". We discovered earlier how the brain constructs our reality. However, it gets more complicated than this. We have our external reality, but we also have our internal reality, which houses our imagination and memories. Most of us are aware of our external reality, but many of us are less aware of our inner world, and this is where our fears and limiting beliefs come from.

When we are creating our external reality, we are laying down a map that is specific to us. This is based on the sensory data that is coming in, and which has been filtered through our primary senses. We don't notice everything and are only aware of a small part of what is going on. As you read this book, you may find that your mind occasionally wanders, and this is perfectly normal. You may have other thoughts that come into your mind. As you think about these thoughts, many people construct an internal picture. For others, it may be an internal voice. Sometimes these can start as a feeling. Controlling your thoughts takes a bit of practise. We will look at some methods to do this that are very effective and not just tips in part two.

Some of these thoughts may be random, and some may be related to the material that you're reading in this book. It's perfectly normal to have thoughts coming into your mind. It is when they are negative in nature and spiral out of control that problems occur. You may recall an event while reading this book, or it may be something personal to you. The more vivid the description then the more accurate the imagined picture will be. The brain uses association. You may hear a particular song and are immediately transported back to a particular memory. Advertisers are aware of the power of association. When we see a picture of ice cream, we often want ice cream. This is called "priming".

We access our internal world as we imagine or remember things. When we are accessing our internal world, we technically are in a trance state. This is a perfectly normal occurrence, and we constantly flip between the external and inner world in a series of mini trances. Have you ever driven home and not remembered the journey? Has anyone ever spoken to you and you didn't hear them? Someone may have spoken, but the junction box in your brain did not bring it to consciousness because you were thinking about something else.

Congratulations, you were in a trance! Let's have a look now at how we lay down our memories. For this, we are going to enter the world of NLP or neuro linguistic programming which can be thought of as software for the mind.

Lay It Down

We lay down our memories from interpreting the data that comes in through our five senses. These senses are sight, sound, taste, smell, and feel. We can add to those senses by including a feeling that we had when we laid down the memory. This is difficult to explain. Some people describe this as a summer, Christmas, or a particular childhood memory feeling. Think about how you feel when you hear a song that reminds you of a particular event in your childhood. If the song is important enough, we often get the accompanying feelings we had at the time we created the memory.

We know all thoughts and memories are a lie. We encode or recall a memory from the data that was received through our senses, and we only create an interpretation of the events that took place. Imagine going on a holiday. Each of us pays attention to different things. Two people going on an identical holiday would have a different map or story to tell from it. For some, it may be too hot, while for others it may not be hot enough. Some may love the hotel, others less so. Likewise, we don't all like the same food, drink, holidays or vacations or choice of partner.

CODING OUR REALITY

Although we process information through our five senses, we all have a preferred sense that we use to recall memories and construct future ones. For example, for some, it may be a feeling, for others, they may recall an image or a sound. It may be an internal voice. This does not mean that we will always use just one particular sense, but there is often one that we prefer. Let's look at these now.

Representational Systems

Visual - Images
Auditory - Sounds
Auditory Digital - Talking to ourselves
Kinaesthetic – Feelings & Touch
Olfactory - Smell
Gustatory - Taste

While we use all of these representational systems, most of us have a preferred or dominant system, which is known as the "lead representational system". This is not a conscious choice, and it takes place at an unconscious level. The breakdown in representational systems as an approximate is:

Visual - 40% of the population.
Kinaesthetic (feeling) - 40% of the population.
Auditory - 20% of the population.
Gustatory (taste) - very low proportion of population.
Olfactory (smell) - very low proportion of population.

Where Is the Map?

The data that comes into our brains is used to construct our map of the world. No two maps look identical. Each one of us has our map, and this is determined by interpreting the data coming into the brain through the five senses. These five senses are visual, auditory, kinaesthetic (feeling), olfactory (smell) and gustatory (taste). These are referred to as "VAKOG" in the world of NLP or Neuro Linguistic Programming (software for the mind). This data is then generalised, deleted and distorted. There is a phrase that states: "the map is not the territory" and this explains the different perceptions.

It is key to understand this, and it explains why nobody thinks that they are being awkward, weird or difficult. It is always amusing to listen to two politicians of different political persuasions arguing. They are both correct, based on their maps of the world!

We have learned how memories and negative thoughts are laid down historically. Let's look at an example of how we lay them down when we think of the future.

Imagined or Real

We are going to explore imagined versus reality now. This example is taken from the author's book "Inside the Mind of Sales".

I'd like you to think about a lemon and imagine holding that lemon in your hand. Notice the bright yellow colour and firmness of the lemon as you gently squeeze it, feeling its waxy surface. Bring the lemon slowly up to your nose, breathe in and noticed the faint smell of lemon. Now take the lemon and place it on a cutting board. Reach across, and grab a very sharp knife. Begin slowly slicing the lemon gently with the knife and notice how the lemon juice drips gently out from the lemon. You may even hear a sound as the lemon juice escapes. Notice the fresh clean smell of lemon as you breathe in. Keep on cutting so that the lemon splits into two halves. Now, cut a wedge of lemon. Reach down and grab the wedge of lemon and bring it slowly up to your nose. Notice how the smell of lemon gets stronger and stronger the closer that it gets to your nose. Continue bringing the lemon to your nose. Breathe in the fresh, pleasing lemon smell. Now take the lemon and open your mouth and take a big bite.

Many of you will now be salivating. When I have described and used the same story in front of a live audience, many screw their faces up when imagining taking a bite from the imaginary lemon. Of course, there is no lemon. It is purely imaginary.

Many of you may have salivated and some of you may even have screwed your face up in anticipation. This shows the power of imagination. There was no lemon, but you engaged your internal thoughts and had an external reaction. This is important as we express what we are thinking through our external expressions relating to those representational systems. We have already established that the brain cannot tell the difference between something real and something imagined. The fMRI scanning of the brain and the piano playing experiment demonstrated this, as discussed in Chapter 5.

What's Your Strategy?

What's your strategy for negative thinking? How do you do it? This may seem like an unusual thing to be discussing. However, everything we do involves a strategy. When we get up from a chair, it doesn't just happen magically. There has to be the intention to move. Various muscles contract and relax to ensure that the movement occurs. The same thing happens with negative thinking. There is a trigger which starts the negative thinking process.

THE EYES HAVE IT

Our eyes play an important role in accessing and creating memories. Through eye movements, we access different parts of our representational systems or senses. We will explore later how to use these for better effect in the second part of the book, where we look at strategies to eliminate negative thinking.

Look Up, Feel Down

Let's start by keeping things very simple. When we want to recall an image or create an image in our internal world, our eyes will move up. Some people can just defocus their eyes and recall or create images without actually moving their eyes. However, the harder the image is to recall, the more that we will move our eyes.

When people are recalling or creating an emotion or speaking to themselves, their eyes will look down. If you think about somebody who is depressed their head will often be bowed and they will be looking down. Conversely, someone who has just won a sporting event or clinched a big deal will often look up with their head back and their arms and hands raised. There are body positions that correspond to emotions. Have you ever seen someone who is depressed walk with a spring in their step or look up and smile? Finally, when we want to recall or hear a sound, our eyes will move to the side.

When you are having negative thoughts stop and become aware of where your eyes are looking. For many people, this will be looking down as they access feelings.

We will explore more of this in part two, but for now, remember that we look up for visuals and look down for feelings.

CHAPTER 11

Programmed for Negativity

A re we really programmed for negativity? Let's explore this and find out.

We find it easier to register negative events more strongly and easier than positive ones, and to dwell on these. This is also known as "positive, negative asymmetry". It means that we are more likely to react strongly to negative criticism than we are to praise. This can explain why traumas can provoke such an emotional reaction, and also why making a bad first impression can linger. I'm sure many of us have had an argument. Someone may have said something to us, and the negative comments linger and spin around in our minds as we replay the event over and over again. Part of this comes from the Emotional Refractory Period, which we will learn about in Part Two. This negative experience can often override the other positive aspects of the day.

What the Research Says

The research shows that, across many experiences, people focus more on the negative than they do on the positive. We pay more attention to negative outcomes than positive ones and base our decisions on negative experiences rather than positive ones. We also attach greater weight to negative outcomes than positive ones. Our learning is disproportionately influenced by negative, rather than positive events.

Words Have Power

We can change people's perspectives and their mental and physical states just from the words that we choose to use. We attempt to communicate our reality by using words. If you can control somebody's perceptions, then you can control their reality. Let's have a look at the power of words and for this, we're going to look at the research of Dr Masaru Emoto.

Dr Masaru Emoto was a Japanese scientist who revolutionised the idea that thoughts and intentions impact the physical realm. He was one of the most important water researchers the world has known. He studied the scientific evidence of how the molecular structure in water transforms when it is exposed to human words, thoughts, sounds and intentions.

Dr Emoto conducted an experiment over a thirty-day period in which he placed equal amounts of cooked rice into three jars, along with an equal amount of water. He then put labels on two of the jars, indicating how they would be treated. The first jar was labelled "Thank You", and would receive positive messages. The second jar was labelled, "You idiot!", and would receive negative messages. The third jar was the control jar and had no label.

To the jar labelled "Thank You", he said: "Thank you" from the bottom of his heart using an emotion of gratitude. He yelled "You idiot" at the jar labelled, "You Idiot", conveying an emotion of anger and frustration. Finally, the third unlabelled rice jar was ignored, and an emotion of indifference was conveyed.

At the end of the thirtieth day, his observations were recorded. The jar that he thanked every day fermented spectacularly and didn't have any black mould or rotting material growing from it. The jar that he yelled and took out his anger on had turned black and was covered in mould. However, the jar that he had ignored for thirty days had even more black mould in it than the jar labelled "You Idiot". According to Dr Emoto, the rice in the jar had rotted.

With his findings, Dr Emoto argued that the power of thoughts and words could change realities, which affect our health, both mental and physical. While this may seem far-fetched, however, if true, what effect could your negative internal voice have on you? It is perhaps worth thinking about this.

The Effect On the Brain

Psychologist John Cappioppa conducted an experiment where the participants were shown pictures that were either positive, neutral or negative. The electrical activity in the brain was then measured. The researchers found that negative images produced much stronger responses than positive or neutral images as measured in the cerebral cortex. This negative bias also applies to bad news, which we are more likely to perceive as being truthful, as opposed to good news.

Bad news stimulates emotions more strongly. One study by J. Kiley Hamlin et al. found that infants as young as three months old show signs of negativity bias when making social evaluations of others. This negativity bias can affect both our personal and business relationships as we disproportionately attach a greater weight to the negative.

Nobel Prize winning researchers, Kahneman and Tversky, discovered that when people make decisions, they consistently place a greater weight on negative aspects of a potential outcome than they do on positive ones. When there is the possibility of either gaining a fixed amount of money or losing the same amount of money, the potential of loss weighs heavier in people's minds. People have a stronger emotion about losing $20 than they do from gaining $20.

From my own experience, I remember going to a cash dispensing machine. I put the card in intending to take out some money from my bank. I was distracted, and I walked away without taking the money. I can remember vividly exactly when and where it was, and putting my card in and punching in the number. I can even remember what the weather was like, despite it being a long time ago. Such is the power of loss.

However, I have been at horse racing events where I have had a small gamble, and won money, and yet I can't remember how much, or any details. This is in contrast to the memory of forgetting to take the money from the cash dispensing machine which is still very vivid.

Negative Bias Examples

Let's have a look at some examples of negative bias. Assume that you have just had your annual review. Let's also assume that there were ten points that you were being measured on as part of an evaluation. Imagine that for eight of those ten points you were deemed excellent, but for two of them, you were scored less. We tend to focus on the two parts that we were weak on, rather than the eight parts that we were strong on. This can often fester in our minds, and we may even discuss our review with somebody else saying: "I can't believe that they said I was underperforming in this area". Therefore, if evaluating somebody, it is always better to sandwich the negative part in the middle between the two positives to lessen the impact.

Financial advisors may have experienced a similar effect when discussing a portfolio of investments with their clients. A sensible investment portfolio combines different investments that all perform well and at different times, so that, on average, the portfolio of investments provides a better risk adjusted return than one investment in isolation. Let's assume that the financial advisor's client has a portfolio of ten mutual funds or collective investments. Let's also assume that nine out of the ten are performing well and one isn't. The reaction of the client is typically to point to the one that isn't doing well and say: "What's wrong with that"?

Let's use another example. Suppose that you have been at a party, had too much to drink and behaved inappropriately. You may even have said something that you wish you hadn't. This can often fester in our minds. However, now knowing how the brain works, most other people will have long forgotten the episode. Let's explore this.

They Won't Remember

Something has to be monumental for people to remember it. If you had watched a sports game or a soap opera on television last night, and I was to ask you what happened, you would probably be able to remember some of it. The memory becomes hazier if I asked you a week later. If I was to ask you a month later, it becomes even hazier. This is if you can remember the game or the soap opera episode at all. I want to share a story to illustrate just how little people remember what we have said.

I once attended an event with an investment company that I worked for. We were one of twelve companies presenting over two days. Each of the companies presenting had its own designated room to present from. Delegates from the conference would attend a selection of ten presentations over two days, by moving from room to room. Each presentation lasted around forty five minutes and there was a break to allow for movement between the rooms, and for coffee.

After the event, I contacted each of the delegates that had attended our presentation to obtain feedback. As I was working my way through the delegate list, there was one delegate that I could not speak to. He went on holiday, or vacation, immediately after the presentation for a week. When I learned of this, I put a note in my diary to contact him on his return, a week later. When I finally spoke to him and asked him what he thought of our presentation. His reply startled me.

"Was I at your presentation?"

It amazed me that he could not remember being at our presentation as our presenter was very good. However, just thinking about this made me realise just how poor human recall is. I suppose that this is understandable if compared to other situations.

Using This Bias

We know people are hard wired for negativity and for "loss aversion" (feeling the pain of loss more than an equivalent gain), and the psychological research backs this up. We are less motivated when an argument is presented as being able to gain something as opposed to when the argument is framed as helping to avoid losing something. Marketers and salespeople realise this and know that you will have greater success if you can remove a pain or a problem than by making somebody better at something. From this also comes "FOMO" or the fear of missing out. Many people have strong emotions when someone passes away, even if they did not know them very well. It is the sense of loss that triggers the emotion. Knowing that this is how we are wired can help put some of our negative thinking into context. It's our neurology at work, and we will look at changing it in Part Two.

Everyone wants to be happy, and let's see now what the science says about happiness.

CHAPTER 12

Science of Happiness

W e all have a desire to be happy, and negative thinking can hold us back. In this chapter, we are going to be exploring what the research says about being happy. We will find out if there are some easy steps that we can take to improve our happiness. In this chapter, I will draw on the work of Professor Richard Wiseman, who has researched this topic extensively to separate fact from fiction, and the reader is referred to Professor Wiseman's excellent publications.

Does Success Lead To Happiness?

Sonja Lyubomirsky at the University of California has reviewed hundreds of studies in which selected people were "cheered up" by experimenters, and then monitored. Researchers used an assortment of procedures to make people feel happy, including positive affirmations, smelling fresh cut flowers, dancing, watching a film, and eating chocolate cake. Other techniques included exaggerating how well volunteers had done on an IQ test, and allowing them to "accidentally" find money on the street that had been placed there.

The results were interesting and showed that happiness doesn't flow from success, it causes it. Happiness makes people more sociable and less selfish, and increases how much people like themselves and others. The by-product of this is that conflicts are more readily resolved, and people have more successful relationships and careers, and are healthier and live longer.

Does More Money Make You Happier?

Most people assume that more money will make them happier. However, it is not the money, but what we do with the money that affects our wellbeing.

In the 1970s, Philip Brickman, from Northwest University and his colleagues, investigated happiness when financial dreams come true. Brickman compared the happiness of those who had won a major prize in the Illinois State lottery together with a control group. His findings concluded that there was no difference in happiness.

Research examining a link between salary and happiness shows the same pattern. A survey by Ed Diener of the University of Illinois and colleagues showed that even those on the Forbes 100 list of wealthiest people are only slightly happier than the average American. The conclusion to be drawn is that when people can afford the necessities in life, an increase in income does not result in being significantly happier.

Why is There No Increase in Happiness?

If we think back to Chapter 5, when we explored the brain, we made reference to suddenly encountering someone wearing a gorilla outfit, and how we pay attention to things that are unusual and novel. People will often head toward a new bar or restaurant when it opens out of curiosity. If we buy a bigger house or a new car, it can provide a short-term boost, but we soon become accustomed to it, and we go back to our pre-purchase level of happiness once the novelty wears off. As the psychologist, David Myers highlights: "Thanks to our capacity to adapt to ever greater fame and fortune, yesterday's luxuries can soon become today's necessities and tomorrow's relics." Some commentators have suggested that fifty per cent of our sense of happiness is determined by our genetics. Some have stated that this cannot be altered. This is highly unlikely, and the reader is referred back to Chapter 9 for clarity. To summarise Chapter 9, genes are only the blueprint, and are a potential for an outcome, except in a small percentage of cases.

What Causes Happiness?

A large proportion of happiness is determined to a great extent by our day to day behaviour, interaction and the way we think about others. Some commentators have suggested that you just have to banish negative thoughts from your mind. However, the research suggests that an attempt to suppress this may be more likely to increase rather than decrease negative thoughts.

An experiment, undertaken by Jennifer Borton and Elizabeth Casey at Hamilton College in New York, asked a group of people to describe their most upsetting thoughts about themselves. The group was then split into two. Half of the group were asked to spend the subsequent eleven days trying to remove the thought from their mind. The other half were asked to carry on with life as usual. At the end of each day, the volunteers were asked to indicate how much they had dwelled on their upsetting thoughts. In addition, they were also asked to rate their mood, anxiety level and self-esteem.

The group that was trying to suppress negative thoughts actually thought more about them compared to those carrying on as normal. Those in the group that were attempting to suppress their thoughts also rated themselves as more anxious, more depressed, and having lower self-esteem. Other research has shown this paradoxical result when asking dieters not to think about chocolate.

Have you ever been unwell or had a part of your body that was sore, and then you became busy and forgot to notice it? I remember when I was a young child having clarinet lessons with a friend of mine. My friend complained of a sore foot to the clarinet teacher. Jokingly, the clarinet teacher said: "I'll stand on your other foot, and you will be too busy worrying about the pain in that foot to notice the pain in the other foot". I always remember that quote because while we don't want to go around standing on other people's feet and causing them harm, it does show the power of distraction. Often if feeling unwell, and lying in bed then this gives plenty of time to think about it, whereas getting up and doing something can cause a distraction. A distraction can provide some immediate relief but will not solve the long term negative thinking. Nonetheless, it is important to be aware of the fact that if you are idle, and allow negative thoughts to creep into your mind, it's not going to benefit you in any way.

This research would seem to suggest that distracting ourselves is one method to reduce negative thinking, and can provide short term relief.

A Problem Shared?

Unpleasant events occur in our lives as part of everyday living. Many people believe that the best way forward is to share the pain with someone else. Research shows that ninety per cent of people believe talking to someone else about the experience will help ease the pain.

Emmanuelle Zack and Bernard Reme, at the University of Louvain in Belgium, carried out a study to investigate this. Volunteers were asked to recall "the most negative, upsetting and emotional event in their lives. They were to recall something that they still thought about, and needed to talk about. They were then divided into two groups.

The first group was to speak to a supportive individual as part of the experiment about the event. The second group was to talk about a more mundane topic, such as a typical day. Volunteers were asked to complete various questionnaires that measured their emotional wellbeing after a week, and then again after two months.

When the results were analysed, those discussing the traumatic event believed that their discussions had been helpful. The questionnaire, however, showed that the discussion had no significant effect. It suggested that speaking to a sympathetic but untrained individual, and trying to suppress negative thoughts is just a waste of time.

If this is not effective, is there something else that is more effective? We will look at this now.

Expressive Writing

There's something magical about writing something down. While thoughts are important, writing something down enables structure, clarity and focus to be given to the thoughts.

In one study volunteers were asked to write about how they felt emotionally about their job loss, and to reflect on their deepest thoughts and feelings about their job loss, including how it had affected both their personal and professional lives. Upon analysis, the results showed participants experienced a remarkable boost in their psychological and physical well-being. This included a reduction in health problems and an increase in both self-esteem and happiness. This can perhaps be explained as follows. Writing something down encourages a more structured and logical process, and while thoughts alone can be random, illogical and unstructured, writing things down can often trigger the brain into looking for solutions. Sometimes simply talking can lead to confusion.

We are now going to look at another powerful wellbeing contributor, gratitude.

Gratitude

Gratitude is a very important psychological aspect which can help with negative thinking. We take many things in life for granted. If you present somebody with a constant sound, image, or smell, something unusual happens. The person slowly gets more and more used to it, and eventually, it vanishes from their awareness. Gratitude is an important aspect to develop in your life as nobody likes spending time with people who are negative.

Write It Down

Many people advocate a gratitude journal. We have already discovered the power of writing things down. It is a good habit to get into, as it forces us to think about things that we are grateful for. This has the effect of putting things in context. The glass is never half full or half empty as was discovered earlier.

The correct description is that it contains fifty per cent air and fifty per cent liquid. You may feel that you are not as popular or as successful in various aspects of your life as you would like to be. Everybody always wants to have more of and to be better at something. I don't know anyone that doesn't. This desire for more doesn't just have to be physical, it can be spiritual or the desire for a type of relationship. Focusing on things that you don't have causes negative feelings. Writing down what you are grateful for in a gratitude journal forces your mind to focus on the things that you do have, and the things that you have achieved.

There are always going to be people who appear to have a better life. This illusion is perpetuated by social media. However, in my experience, very rarely does someone have everything in balance. They may be financially successful, however, there may be problems with their health, family or their relationship.

Just as a camera has a narrow field of view, so do our perceptions, and we don't always see the true picture when comparing ourselves to others. I was surprised to learn that one of my favourite iconic rock singers, from one of my favourite bands, had been in therapy for many years. As a child, I idolised this individual and the group. I had always assumed that this individual had a perfect life and one that I would have loved to have had.

As gratitude is such a powerful force there is a special chapter dedicated to it in Part Two.

Plotting the Journey

Visualisation is an important tool when we want to achieve something. We have seen that it is the same part of the brain that is involved with visualising something as with actually doing it. Some people say that they have difficulty creating mental pictures, and that they can't do it. This is always an interesting statement as I wonder how do people remember where they have parked their car. We can all visualise things just to differing degrees. However, when we talk about visualisation, this also means a feeling that may occur, or perhaps it is a sound. This is all included in the expression "visualisation".

In a study carried out by Laura King at Southern Methodist University, volunteers were divided into three groups. In the first group, sixteen volunteers spent a few minutes for four consecutive days describing their ideal future. They were asked to be realistic but to imagine a positive outcome, and achieving their goals. The second group was asked to imagine a traumatic event that had happened to them, and the third group simply wrote their plans for the day. The results revealed that those who had described their best possible future ended up significantly happier than those in the other groups.

A key differentiator for people who have achieved success and change in their lives is from taking action. There has been much written about the law of attraction, however, simply sitting and meditating is unlikely to get us any results without some form of action. The unconscious mind will help and direct us, but we need action. There are going to be many exercises and strategies that you can use in Part Two of this book to help reduce and eliminate negative thinking. However, if you don't do these exercises, and just rely on reading this book, then the probability of success is much lower. After all, you wouldn't learn to play the piano by just reading a music book, would you?

Benefits of a Loving Relationship

Being in a loving relationship is not only good for our mental but also our physical health. If not in a relationship, then being kind and loving to ourselves helps our wellbeing. The big question is, does this come from expressing love, receiving love, or both.

An experiment by Kory Floyd from Arizona State University asked some volunteers to think about someone they loved, and then to spend twenty minutes writing about why this person meant so much to them. A second group was asked to write about something that happened to them during the last week as the control in the experiment.

Over the next five weeks, both groups repeated the exercise three times. The results showed that there was a marked increase in happiness and a decrease in stress and cholesterol levels in the first group.

To Give Is To Receive

Many negative thinkers use retail therapy as a solution. Buying a new pair of shoes or the latest gadget may make you feel much better, but is this the wisest way to spend your money, and how long will you derive pleasure from this?

Psychologists Leaf van Boven and Thomas Gilovich conducted some research to find out which was most likely to generate the greatest feeling of happiness. They wanted to compare buying goods against buying an experience.

An experiment was devised in which they divided people into two groups. One group was to recall an object that they had recently bought, and the other group was to describe an experiential purchase. Both were asked to rate their mood on two scales. One scale measured bad to good, and the other scale measured sad to happy.

The results from the experiment showed that both in terms of short and long term happiness, the experiences that were purchased made people feel better than buying the goods. There is a reason for this and you may be familiar with the expression "rose tinted glasses." We have already mentioned that all memories are a lie, and are merely our interpretation of an event which has been filtered through our primary senses.

There is another powerful reason, Positive experiences promote happiness inducing behaviours. This includes spending time with others. I remember when I was younger we used to holiday on the west coast of Scotland. My parents had bought a small speedboat for us to use to water ski. It was great fun being out in the speedboat, and it was even more fun when my friends were there too. It's the memories of being in the boat with my friends that I recall the most and not the times when I was out in the boat on my own.

The issue with buying goods is that it can cause jealousy in others who are unable to afford the same item. This can result in a feeling of self isolation.

Many lottery winners blow all or most of their winnings. If someone suddenly receives a large sum of money, then their lifestyle changes, and they have to adapt to the lifestyle that goes with it. This can alienate previous friends and acquaintances who are unable to participate in this new lifestyle. This can cause cognitive dissonance in the winners, between the social circle that they find themselves in now, and where they feel they belong. The unconscious mind will do its best to solve this problem and removes the perceived problem which is the newly acquired wealth, to restore the status quo. We have read about people returning to their old job in a factory after blowing all the lottery money and being much happier without it.

Altruism Trumps

Research by Elizabeth Dunn, from the University of British Columbia, has established that focusing on ourselves can have a detrimental effect on our happiness. An experiment was devised where participants were divided randomly into two groups. Participants were given an envelope containing either $5 or $20 and were asked to spend the money by 5 p.m. that evening. One group was instructed to spend the money on themselves, while the other group was asked to spend the money on someone else.

Against expectations, the participants who spent money on friends and family found themselves being significantly happier.

William Harbor, from the University of Oregon, conducted an experiment where he gave participants $100 in a virtual bank account, and then scanned brain activity. The participants saw some of their money being given to help those in need via taxation. They were then asked to either donate the rest of the money or keep it for themselves. The results from the scan showed that the caudate nucleus and the nucleus accumbens in the brain became active when participants saw some of the money going to those in need. Both were even more active when participants voluntarily donated the money. These two brain regions also spring into action when our basic needs are satisfied such as when we feel valued by others, or when we eat enjoyable food. This seems to establish a direct brain link between helping others and happiness. Scientifically speaking, if you want retail therapy, then spend your money on other people.

Happiness in Kindness

Researcher, Sonja Lubomirsky organised an experiment for a group of participants to engage in acts of kindness, of a non-financial nature, each week for six weeks. These included things such as writing a thank you note, helping a friend, and giving blood to others. The group was divided in half, with one group performing one act of kindness a day, while others conducted all five acts of kindness. The ones who performed the one act of kindness recorded a small increase in happiness, while those who carried out all acts of kindness increased their happiness by forty per cent.

In this book, we are trying to remove the hearsay and focus on scientific evidence that supports various claims. Science shows us that indulging in acts of kindness toward others, and spending money on them will benefit us in the long term. Yet everyone is selfish. You may say: "Well, I know somebody who is very unselfish and they always give to charity, or they get involved in charitable activities". However, every action undertaken by humans is due to a feeling, to either get more of a feeling or less of it. While giving to charities and getting involved in charity work is commendable, the reason that people do it is that it makes them feel good. Perhaps charity workers know something that many of us don't.

The Company of Others

Research by Richburg in 1998, showed that having more close friendships has been associated with a nineteen per cent greater life satisfaction, and a twenty three per cent greater sense of optimism.

In 2001, Prezza showed that positive thoughts about neighbours has been associated with a sixteen per cent increase in happiness, and twenty five per cent less likelihood of experiencing feelings of loneliness.

Chaeyoon Lin and Robert Putnam found that in religious groups, irrespective of faith, having ten friends or liked minded people is the optimum number, and this correlates to happiness.

Achieving Something

According to research by Orlick in 1998, people who achieve a steady flow of minor accomplishments report an increase in life satisfaction by twenty two per cent, compared to those who only focus on major accomplishments.

A study by Meulemann in 2001 found that the ability to continue trying, despite suffering setbacks, has been associated with a more optimistic outlook on life. This was shown in thirty one per cent of people studied. In addition, forty two per cent of people reported greater life satisfaction.

Another study by Ryan and Dziurawiec in 2001 found that people whose values were the most materialistic rated their lives as the least satisfying.

In this chapter, we have looked at the science behind happiness, and for many of us, simply reflecting on these findings, and changing behaviour, outlook and mindset, may be enough. If this does not apply to you, don't be concerned. We have some powerful methods coming up later.

Let's now move on to how to motivate ourselves to take action, which, for many of us, can be a challenge.

CHAPTER 13

Influencing Yourself

We have already discovered the importance of language and the power of words. We can now use the power of language on ourselves. In the author's earlier work, it was pointed out that we should try to avoid the question word "why" when asking questions. Let's revisit this topic.

The reason to avoid this in everyday conversation is that asking "why" questions causes people to justify their behaviour and rationalise it. If I said:

"Why did you buy that car?"

It comes across as questioning your criteria and values, and the selection process for buying that car. When asked "why", people tend to justify their behaviour. We can, however, use the "why" question when we want to know somebody's process for doing something. We can couple this with the word "might", for a powerful effect. I'm drawing here on work from Michael Pantalon's book "Instant Influence".

All change comes from within. The first thing to establish is the motivation for change. This includes assessing ourselves. If a hypnotist asks a client what is their motivation on a scale of one to ten, with 10 being the largest, they pay close attention to the answer. If the client says it is a three out of ten, then the client might as well just go home. There must be a motivation to change.

We will look at the steps that Michael Pantalon advises going through when influencing and motivating ourselves shortly. Before we do this, let's examine three guiding principles first. These are derived from work by psychologists including, Jack and Sharon Brehm, Martin Seligman, Leon Festinger and Daryl Bem.

The Principles

1. No one has to do anything. The choice always resides with the individual.
2. Everyone already has enough motivation.
3. Focusing on small components of motivation works much better than asking about resistance.

From this, we have a series of steps that take the form of questions. (Notice the use of the word "might" in **Step 2.** This is an important word to use).

The Steps

Step 1

State what you wish to change and define this in terms of behaviour, not results? For example:

"I want to have control over my negative thinking."

Rather than,

"I want to have no negative thoughts."

Step 2

Why **might,** you want to change your negative thinking? Write down your answer. It is best if this is the first thing that comes to mind without trying to analyse or evaluate your answer. There is something magical about writing something down. Keep writing until you feel you have covered everything. Don't be concerned if you wander off-topic.

Step 3

How ready are you to change? If there was a scale between **1** and **10,** where **1** means "not ready at all" and **10** means "totally ready", what number would you pick?

Whatever number you select, ask yourself:

"Why didn't I pick a lower number?"

Write down this answer. If you said a **1,** then either ask the same question again, but this time select a smaller step toward change. You can also ask, what would it take to turn **1** into a **2**?

Step 4

Imagine you've changed. What would the positive outcomes or benefits be? Write down your answer.

Step 5

Why are those outcomes important to you? Or what's important to you about....?

Step 6

What's the next step, if any?

If you have gone through this exercise thoroughly, notice how your thinking has changed. This clever technique gets people to resist themselves and can be used in business, therapy and sales.

Difficulty Taking Action

If we are trying to change, it can often feel overwhelming. The key is to focus on small steps or goals, on taking action, and not on outcomes.

This process will help motivate you to change if you are not already fully there. You can use this method to help with motivation, and use the techniques and exercises.

We will now move to the practical exercises in Part Two.

PART TWO

Tools for Change

INTRODUCTION TO PART TWO

In this part of the book, we are going to look at powerful techniques that we can use to help eliminate unwanted negative thinking. Human beings are complicated, and there will be certain techniques that will work better for some, more than others. If something works for you great, if not, don't dwell on it. Simply try another technique until you find one that works best for you. We don't all like the same sports, music and food, and we can't expect everything to work for everyone.

The degree of success that you have will depend on your desire for change, your willingness to use these techniques, and your ability to absorb yourself in the experience.

Some techniques that we are going to be looking at may seem unusual to some and are very different to conventional methods, and I would simply ask that you keep an open mind.

Remember, the conscious critical mind does analysis. It will want to critique and evaluate the techniques and say that they can't possibly work. If your conscious mind was so good at providing a solution, it would have done so by now, and you

126

would not be reading this book. It has had its chance. Now it is time to try something else.

Therefore, let's suspend critical judgement, and use methods that just work. We want results, not intellectual chess. If you are not comfortable with one technique or method, simply move on. Remember the mantra, if it works for you great, if not, try something else. Try to suspend any disbelief, and just go along with the experience, just like we do at a cinema or movie theatre. When we go to see a film or a movie, we don't sit there and say: "This image is not real, it is just pixels on a screen and is a two dimensional entity". We suspend disbelief and just immerse ourselves in the movie.

Cast your mind back to earlier chapters in the first part of the book, where we discussed reality and belief. The scientific evidence hopefully will have challenged many of the beliefs that you may have had about what is possible.

These techniques that we will discuss have worked very effectively for many people. As the unconscious mind is the powerhouse, let's start first with the very powerful "Deep Trance Identifier" or DTI method.

CHAPTER 14

Unconscious Access Using DTI

Deep Trance Identifier Program

The first technique that we are going to learn speaks directly to the unconscious mind. You can learn to do this yourself after some practise. For ease, I have recorded a special audio program where all you have to do is nothing, other than listen and use your imagination. If you have not downloaded the audio already, please do so now. The audio is a specially recorded Rapid Learning Accelerator DTI programme that speaks directly to your unconscious mind. The link is here. www.eliminatenegativethinking.com*

Background

Deep Trance Identification (DTI) is an unconscious process in which someone is guided into experiencing the world as if they were another person. It is a relaxing experience, and it has enabled people to develop new abilities. It was first developed in Russia as a tool to increase the musical abilities of violin players, and has been tested under double-blind experiments. It works by allowing people to get out of the way of themselves, and to step into and identify with someone else. This may seem unbelievable and I would simply ask that you suspend any judgement and just roll with it.

DTI is one of the most powerful processes for personal generative and therapeutic change. It is a very powerful tool, and is used by many successful individuals, including sports and business people. The audio will guide you into a relaxed state, and all you have to do is find a quiet place, and pop on your earphones or headphones. Then simply allow the sounds and words to drift past you, and do nothing. Just suspend your disbelief in the same way that you do when in a movie theatre or cinema.

As this audio targets the powerhouse that is the unconscious mind, it is best used frequently and ideally at least once a day for thirty days. There will be changes, and they will be subtle. This is arguably one of the most powerful methods, and when combined with the other conscious methods, provides a platform for change. Once you get familiar with the process, you can do it yourself.

*DO NOT USE THIS AUDIO WHEN DRIVING, OPERATING MACHINERY, OR WHEN FULL CONSCIOUS AWARENESS IS REQUIRED.

DO NOT USE THIS AUDIO IF YOU SUFFER FROM EPILEPSY OR MENTAL ILLNESS AND PLEASE CONSULT WITH YOUR DOCTOR IF IN ANY DOUBT.

We will now move on to the conscious mind methods, starting with some of the basics before moving to some of the more advanced techniques. Let's start with diet and exercise.

CHAPTER 15

Diet & Exercise

Diet and exercise are two of the most basic things that we can change in the process of eliminating negative thinking. This may seem quite basic, however, we want to stack as many things as we can in our favour. We must have solid foundations before moving on to some of the more advanced methods.

WE ARE WHAT WE EAT

Numerous studies have extolled the virtues of a good diet and an exercise regime. Some commentators have even listed this as a panacea. There is little doubt that improving our diet, and engaging in an exercise regime will improve our wellbeing. However, we all know people with terrible diets who don't engage in exercise, and who are incredibly positive, so it is not the whole story.

Simply engaging in exercise and changing diet on its own is unlikely to completely eliminate negative thinking. It may help, and if it does great. Rather than dismissing this as being less important, we're going to investigate how improving your diet and exercise can enhance mental wellbeing. Depending on the extent of negative thinking, or outlook, this on its own may show immediate improvements.

Exercise releases feel good endorphins, such as dopamine and serotonin. Exercising also enhances blood circulation in the body and can help with symptoms of stress when under pressure. Further studies have shown that exercise can improve cognitive processes, and can help with sleep disorders. This does not mean that you have to indulge in very strenuous cardio vascular exercise for thirty minutes a day to reap the benefits. Simply going for a brisk walk that elevates your heart rate will provide significant benefits.

For many of us, the thought of having to alter our diet, and eliminate all our favourite foods and then spend hours in the gym is not appealing. The truth regarding exercise is that you don't have to spend hours in the gym. Let's look at how we can "cheat exercise" without breaking out in a sweat, and then how we can "cheat a diet".

Cheating Exercise

While I enjoy going to the gym and lifting weights, I'm less keen on spending a lot of time on cardio machines. When I wanted to lose weight and get the benefits of doing light cardio exercise, without having to spend lots of time in the gym, I simply increased the amount of walking that I did. When we are walking, we don't get such a high heart rate compared to vigorous cardio vascular activity, but it still rises. I always found it rather amusing when I was at the gym that many people would drive to the gym to run on the treadmill, and then drive home. This is understandable on a cold dark winter's evening, but in the height of summer, it seemed rather strange.

Most people are unaware that you burn almost the identical amount of calories whether you walk or run a mile or kilometre. Knowing this, I developed a technique that I call "cheating exercise". Rather than going on a big long walk all at once, I aimed to increase the amount of walking that I would do throughout the day. This was measured using a step measuring device. Let me give you an example of this.

Human beings are naturally quite lazy, and we all like to conserve energy. You can see this if you go to park your car at a supermarket, hypermarket or shopping mall. Everybody drives around to find the nearest possible space. Knowing that most people do this, I would deliberately park as far away from the entrance to the store as possible in the car park or parking lot. This would mean that I would get an extra few minutes of walking. It had the added benefit of meaning that my car was unlikely to be damaged by somebody opening their door.

Other ways of cheating exercise include taking the stairs instead of the lift or elevator. If taking the stairs to the fourteenth floor, you would need legs like a gorilla, however, getting off at the twelfth floor and then walking up the last two floors is manageable. Simply creating opportunities to walk, and taking the stairs instead of the lift, or elevator can enable extra exercise to be carried out without even noticing it. We can easily get off the bus one stop early or park our car slightly further away, and the extra short walk is hardly noticeable.

Many of us are busy, and are time constrained. If you work in an office and there is a sandwich shop across from your office, instead of walking directly to it, simply take a detour to the shop. This may only take a minute more. However, if your target is to have 30 minutes of walking activity a day, then you have just covered at least one thirtieth of it by going to get a sandwich!

As exercise contributes towards mental wellbeing, and with it a positive mood and a positive mental attitude, this seemed to me to be a sensible solution rather than having to spend thirty to sixty minutes on a treadmill or a machine.

It's very easy to make excuses to avoid exercise. However, doing it this way means that we don't break out in a sweat, and we get the benefits of light exercise, which will benefit your health and your wellbeing.

Diet

Diet is always a hot topic of debate, and there are always new diets and fads appearing. As this topic is complicated and ever-evolving, and with many differing views, the reader is advised to check out the current material, and the latest research on the subject for more details.

As mentioned, there are people we know who have terrible diets, and who don't drink enough water or take enough exercise. In many cases, they are no stranger to a beer or a glass of wine, and yet are very positive. So diet and exercise are not a panacea.

Committing to changing our diets shows taking action and is a step towards eliminating our negative thinking. Different food substances can affect mood and energy levels, and one thing that we can agree on is that natural food is better for us than processed food. Another thing that everybody agrees on is that excess sugar in a diet is not good for us. I get a headache if there is too much sugar in my diet!

It is generally considered the Mediterranean diet is one of the healthier ones. However, we all differ in what we can eat, and how it affects us. That being said, my late father had a saying that if we have everything in moderation, we won't go too far wrong. This will apply to most people. It is the excess that usually causes the problems.

Keeping things simple, if we reduce the amount of processed food, and in particular added refined sugar from our diet this is beneficial. Increasing our consumption of vegetables, particularly green vegetables, and an assortment of protein sources, including fish and meat, should serve us well. Further enhancements can include incorporating nuts, grains and fruit. Adding vitamin supplements to a diet can make up for any shortfall, particularly vitamin D, which can become depleted in the winter months when living in some countries.

One of the issues with excessive sugar consumption is that people can suffer from a sugar crash and become lethargic. Too much sugar in the bloodstream causes insulin to be released, which reduces the blood sugar level in response. This can result in a sugar craving, and eating more sugar to top this level back up again. Something that I learned that has benefited me when training is to pay attention to the glycaemic index of carbohydrate foods. The higher the glycaemic index, the easier the carbohydrate is converted into sugar in the bloodstream. A lower glycaemic index means that it takes longer to digest the carbohydrate. Lower glycaemic foods are less likely to cause a sudden sugar surge into the bloodstream. If you are a fruit lover, consider incorporating berries into your diet such as strawberries or blueberries, as these will give you the fruit taste, and benefit from a lower glycaemic index.

We are all different and different things work for different people. If diet is a particular topic of interest, it is worth seeking the advice of a qualified professional or doing some research on the subject. I will add one particular caveat here, there are many views and opinions on what constitutes the ideal diet. From my own research, I found this to be a minefield. That being said, I know that if I remove processed food, and food high in sugar, I immediately feel better, more alert and more motivated. It is worth experimenting with different diets to see what works best for you. Many people have strong opinions on diets, and may not eat particular food types. It is a large topic to cover, and experimenting will uncover what is best for you.

"Cheating" a Diet

Changing our diet, just like a habit, can be hard to do. Too much sugar can cause a sugar crash, and we can feel hungry again. This can become a vicious cycle. However, we also get a dopamine rush from sugary foods as the pleasure centres of the brain become activated. This is why sugar can be so addictive. It is no surprise that foods that are high in sugar and fat are the tastiest for many of us. We only have to look at ice cream, which ticks all the boxes, to demonstrate this.

Something that I use, when I'm looking to reduce my sugar and calorie intake, is to increase the amount of protein in my diet. Protein has the effect of being slower to digest and hence makes us feel fuller for longer. Casein is a type of protein and is slower to digest, and you can find this in eggs or buy it as a standalone dietary supplement powder.

I have found that incorporating a greater level of protein into my diet means that I am less keen on snacking on biscuits, chocolates or candy. I lose weight and feel more energetic. You may feel the same too. We are what we eat. Why not try changing your diet and incorporate some walking into your everyday life and notice the difference.

Let's move on now to the powerful and popular Cognitive Behavioural Therapy (CBT) method.

CHAPTER 16

Cognitive Behavioural Therapy (CBT)

Cognitive Behavioural Therapy or CBT evolved from the work of the psychologist Albert Ellis and the psychiatrist Aaron Beck. The idea behind CBT is to encourage people to take responsibility for their thinking, which in return affects their state of mind. It questions how thoughts and triggers in the environment and the surroundings can create feelings. This leads to reactions and symptoms resulting in certain behaviours.

The cognitive behavioural model breaks the problem down into five parts.

1. Thoughts
2. Feelings
3. Physical reactions/symptoms
4. Behaviour
5. Environmental Factors

CBT has been used very effectively in many areas of therapy. Let's explore the ABCDE process you can use to help eliminate negative thinking.

ABCDE Process

1. **A**dversity (trigger). What are the activating situations or thoughts?
2. **B**elief. What belief is held regarding the challenge?
3. **C**onsequences. What happens when the negative thoughts and beliefs are accepted, and what effect does this have on emotional states and outcomes?
4. **D**isputation. What alternative evidence is there that contradicts the belief?
5. **E**nergisation. What alternative thinking can be undertaken?

Research has shown that CBT can be more effective than drugs and conventional psychotherapy. It is particularly successful when used in conjunction with mindfulness and NLP.

Beginning the Process

Let's begin by using CBT to help identify and replace negative thoughts. We are going to be using the "**ABCDE**" method, and reference a one-page document which can be downloaded from the link www.eliminatenegativethinking.com

One of the biggest advantages of writing thoughts down is that it helps to clarify them as they occur, rather than to have an uncontrolled flow of thoughts or emotions. If you have not downloaded the document, you can always write down your thoughts and feelings based on the description and table below. If you don't have the document to hand, simply write your thoughts in a small notebook or mobile device.

The best thing to do is to write these negative thoughts down as they are occurring. We have seen in earlier chapters just how quickly memory can fade and how inaccurate our recall can be.

If you prefer and to make it even easier for you, a printed journal is available at mybook.to/ENTJournal. In order to help simplify the process, the following description is based on the Table 1 below.

A	**Activating Event** (Trigger)	What triggered an emotion? E.g. Event image, memory sensation, someone else.	Emotions Rated 0-10
B	**Belief** & Thoughts About **A**	What thoughts did you have? E.g. About you, situation, others or future	Describe
C	**Consequences** of A & B On Emotions and feelings	What emotion did you feel?	Emotions (Describe)
			Behaviour (Describe)
D	**Dispute** Question Examine Explore Alternatives	Write down an alternative for each thought in **B**	Describe
E	**Effect** of Alternative Beliefs	How do you feel or what action to take from **D**	Emotions Re-rated 0-10
			New or Alternative Action

Table 1

We are going to start with the C heading first. This is the consequences heading.

Consequences Box

Step 1. Under this heading write down how you are feeling and the emotion accompanying it. Some examples of typical emotions are listed below:

1. Anger
2. Anxiety
3. Depression
4. Envy
5. Guilt
6. Jealousy
7. Shame

Step 2. After naming the emotion, beneath it write down how you responded or what you felt like doing. Some examples are listed:

1. Avoided someone or something.
2. Became withdrawn or felt isolated.
3. Became aggressive.
4. Escaped from a situation.
5. Procrastinated and did not take action.
6. Sought reassurance or endorsement.
7. Became defensive.

Activating (or Trigger) Box

Step 3. In the activating or trigger box, describe the event that has caused the unhelpful thoughts or feelings. Some examples are:

1. Remembered something in the past.
2. Anticipated something in the future.
3. Something occurring now.
4. Something imagined in your mind.
5. Experienced a physical sensation.
6. Experienced a strong emotional response.
7. Identified with a situation.
8. Linked an event to someone else.

Beliefs

Step 4. Under the beliefs heading, describe the meaning you have attributed to the activating event (trigger) when you felt the emotion. E.g. "Now everyone knows that I'm a failure." Describe in as much detail as you can and critically analyse your thoughts. Is there any evidence for your statement?

Dispute

Step 5. Under the dispute heading question the validity of your thoughts. Are you thinking in extreme terms, e.g. all or nothing?

1. Have you invented the worst case scenario?
2. Are you using generalisations like always or never?
3. Are you predicting the future?
4. Are you mind reading people?
5. Are you eliminating positive thinking?
6. Are you negatively focussing on an argument?
7. Are you attaching a self-identifying label to yourself?
8. Are you outsourcing your thinking?
9. Is the comparison to a previous event valid?

Effects Box

Step 6. How do you feel now from the action that you took in **D**. Re-rate how you feel now on a 1-10 scale. What new action will you take or do you need to take?

More and more physicians and psychiatrists are referring their patients for CBT to help overcome a wide range of problems, and the results have been good. CBT can be incorporated with NLP, hypnosis and meditation to increase its effectiveness. As part of my diploma in Clinical Hypnotherapy and NLP, I studied CBT and it is very effective.

Next, we are going to look at goals as another tool, and these can be used to help give us direction and satisfaction in our lives.

CHAPTER 17

Scoring a Goal

Setting goals helps reduce negative thinking and to focus on positive outcomes. I remember early on in my career speaking to somebody who said: "A man without a target hits nothing". That phrase has always stayed with me and is very true. There is another old phrase, "If you don't know where you're going, any old road will take you there". If you don't have a goal or a purpose or something to work towards, then it is a bit like a compass spinning around, and not pointing in any direction.

Many people feel dissatisfaction and have negative emotions. They have thoughts of being a low achiever, and feeling stuck. Someone I know realises the importance of goal setting. She describes it as having something to look forward to. In her case, it is booking the summer holiday or vacation. Equally, if we set our goals too high, and don't achieve them, this can cause a feeling of negativity and failure.

Feel Good Boost

When we want something, and get it, our brains give us a shot of the "feel good" neurotransmitter dopamine. We can use goals to help us eliminate negative thinking, and to feel better about ourselves, and get this dopamine injection. The key is to set small goals that are within our control and that are readily achievable.

This is why "to do lists" are so effective because you get a hit of dopamine every time you tick off an item on the list. People who work in sales and business are aware of how effective this can be. They notice the feeling of accomplishment when an item is completed and ticked off the list.

The research backs this up. In one study by McLeod et al., volunteers participated in three short one hour goal setting and planning sessions online. The researchers compared the results to a control group that didn't complete the exercises. The study established a causal link between goal setting and the wellbeing of the volunteers.

In 1998, Krueger discovered that those who could identify with a goal they were pursuing were nineteen per cent more likely to feel satisfied with their lives, and 26 per cent more likely to feel positive about themselves.

Scoring Good Goals

There are good goals, and there are less helpful goals. Let's look at an example of this. Suppose that you decided that you wanted to write a book.

A good goal would be to set yourself a time limit, and commit to writing fifteen minutes a day, or to set yourself a word target of five hundred words a day. This is within your control and is readily achievable.

An example of a less than helpful goal would be specific numbers which are outside of your control. Let's suppose that you set yourself a target to be a bestselling author or to achieve a specific ranking as compared to other books. This would be a bad goal, as this is out of your control.

When we don't achieve a goal, this can negatively affect us. It is important to make goals realistic and achievable, but not too easy. This doesn't mean that we have to achieve our goal immediately. Seeing progress towards our goals enhances our well being too. Our larger goal may be to write a book, which can seem a daunting prospect. However, writing five hundred words a day is not particularly challenging. Here we get a double hit because we achieve our daily goal, and we are also making progress towards the larger goal.

Examples of goals that you can set yourself would be to achieve a specific minimum number of steps every day when walking, or committing to a thirty minute walk every day. You can also commit to doing the mental exercises that are listed in this book.

It is always worthwhile breaking the main goal down into smaller constituent parts so that we get the dopamine hit as we achieve the smaller goals on the road to achieving the bigger one.

Moving the Goal Posts

It is worth having another goal in mind, after the completion of the current one, to avoid the "void" feeling that can occur when we achieve a goal. It is important to keep revisiting your goals, and revise them as you achieve them. I'm sure many of us have had the situation where we set ourselves a target or a goal. When we achieve it, we can feel slightly at a loss, or even slightly down afterwards. We often wonder what we should aim for next. I remember I set myself a goal to become the manager of the sales team when working for a life insurance company. When I eventually achieved this goal, I was delighted. However, not long afterwards, I felt a bit empty. I had focused so hard on achieving this goal that there was now a void, and I didn't have another goal to aim for.

Using Goals for Eliminating Negative Thinking

Suppose that our goal is to never have a negative thought again. First of all, this is unrealistic, impractical, and could even be a dangerous goal. After all, if somebody asked us to jump off a building, negative thoughts would prevent a potentially disastrous experience.

Our main goal could be to have greater control over our thoughts. Here we are focussing on the process and not the outcome as defined by numbers. Our mini goal on the way to this goal could be to do at least one exercise in this book a day.

ABC of Goals

There are three essential features of goals as established by Frank L Smoll, a psychologist from Washington University. He discovered that the most effective goals are:

1. **A**chievable
2. **B**elievable
3. **C**ommitted

SMART Goals

If you work in business, then you will more than likely have come across "smart goals" previously. Smart is an acronym and the letters stand for:

1. **S**pecific
2. **M**easurable
3. **A**chievable
4. **R**ealistic
5. **T**ime bound

The key point is to take action to start the process. Procrastination only delays this as time slips by, and a feeling of underachievement ensues.

Returning to our analogy relating to writing a book. There are millions of unwritten books out there, as people are always going to write a book, usually at some point in the future. This point often never arrives, and all these books remain unwritten.

Brain Assistance

Have you ever noticed, that if you have bought a new car or pair of shoes you pay attention to other cars or people's shoes? This happens because the Reticular Activating System (RAS) has been activated. The RAS is a cluster of cells located at the base of the brain that processes sensory information related to the things that need our attention right now. The RAS is aware of what we are paying attention to at any moment in time and focuses only on information related to it.

We can use this knowledge knowing that if we are focussing on information related to our goals, then it can help us. This can also work in a negative way too. If we have just broken up with someone, then all we see are couples everywhere enjoying themselves. Our brain plays tricks on us constantly. We can use the tricks to our advantage, and not to our disadvantage.

Let's move on to a key part now, learning to calm our minds.

CHAPTER 18

Quietening the Mind

Quietening the mind and controlling thoughts is a key aspect of controlling and eliminating negative thinking. The link between the mind and the body means that a stressed body results in a stressed mind, and vice versa.

The psychologist Amy Cuddy found that there is a strong link between feelings of power and adopting a power pose. It is not surprising that this takes place because other disciplines, such as yoga, have body positions at their core. This means that by adopting a different body posture it is possible to generate a corresponding emotional response. A relaxed mind means a relaxed body, and vice versa. Before we relax the mind, let's learn to relax the body.

RELAXING THE BODY

Negative thinking is often associated with underlying stress, and this can manifest in the body too. We have seen the importance of thoughts on the body and how this can be detrimental to our health. Many people are so tense that they can't remember how to relax, so we're going to start right at the beginning, and then progress to faster methods as we go through this chapter.

Learning to Relax (Exercise 1)

When learning how to relax, it is important to set a benchmark. For us to perceive something, we need to have contrast and for there to be the diametric opposite. If we don't have light, we can't experience darkness.

Let's begin by providing some contrast as we learn to relax. Put your hand out in front of you and clench your hand to make a fist. Clench it as tightly as possible and squeeze as hard as you possibly can. Hold this for the count of ten and then relax the tension out of your hand fully and completely. Now feel the difference.

Whole Body Relaxation

Once you've done this a few times, let's move on to expanding this feeling of contrast to experience relaxation throughout the whole of your body. This is called a progressive relaxation exercise and we will go through it now.

Whole Body Relaxation (Exercise 2)

There is a complimentary downloadable audio available at www.eliminatenegativethinking.com to assist you.

Your awareness can be moved around. It's very easy to move somebody's awareness. You are now aware of your breathing and the sensations in your mouth. You are now aware of your clothing touching your skin. It's almost impossible to resist this because we have to think about something first to discount it.

We can take advantage of the ability to move our awareness and use this on ourselves. Let's start the exercise.

Find a quiet place to relax. It can be sitting up or lying down. Sitting up is often better, as when lying down, many people can become just a bit too relaxed and end up falling asleep.

Start by tensing the muscles in your scalp. Hold the tension and then relax. Now tense all the muscles in and around your eyes. You may want to scrunch up your eyes to do this. Hold the tension and relax. Now tense the muscles around your cheeks, hold the tension, and then relax fully and completely.

Repeat this process of creating tension and then relaxing as you move through the parts of your body from your jaw, neck, shoulders, upper back, chest, abdomen, lower back, upper arms, hands, upper legs, lower legs and feet. The audio will make this easier for you to do.

DO NOT LISTEN TO THE AUDIO WHEN DRIVING OR WHEN FULL AWARENESS IS REQUIRED

It is worth doing this exercise a few times to experience the difference between tension and relaxation. As you get better at this, you will be able to just focus your awareness on a part of your body, for example, your scalp, and just relax the muscles without having to contract them. You can then do the same as you move through each body part.

RELAXING THE MIND

Having learned how to relax the body, let's move on to relaxing the mind.

The following exercise can be done sitting up or lying down. To avoid drifting off to sleep, it is better to do the exercise sitting up. If you are feeling tired, sprinkle some cold water on your face and take some deep breaths. This will help to reduce tiredness and prevent you from falling asleep. Don't try to force things and get frustrated. Just let things happen.

Stage 1

Relax your body using the techniques listed above, observe the thoughts coming into your mind, and try to contain these. At first, there may be thoughts coming in from everywhere. However, as you practise, then the thoughts will become less chaotic and random until you experience fewer thoughts. The point is not to lose the train of thoughts but to follow them. This ability will vary from person to person. If you have lots of thoughts, the idea is to learn to quieten them. This can be done with practice. Start with one minute and aim for three minutes as you practise. Do this thought controlling exercise at least twice a day for 7 days. If you are struggling for time, and if you are at work or on the move, you can use the bathrooms as your quiet room.

Stage 2

By now your mind will have quietened, and we can move on to the next stage. The purpose here is to hold on to one single thought for a longer period and to banish other thoughts. As we are learning a new skill, this is not going to happen immediately. The more that you do this, the better you will get until you can quieten your mind and focus on one particular thought. One method that can help with focusing your thoughts is to light a candle and to stare at the flame. Really focus on the flame and observe its flickering and its colour. If any other thoughts come to mind, simply focus on the flame again. Keep doing this until you can hold the flame in your mind for at least a few minutes.

Developing this particular skill will make you realise that you have control over your mind and not the other way around. Any thoughts that you do not have control over, control you. At first, you will probably only be able to do this for a few seconds however, as you practise this will become easier. You must be able to concentrate on one single thought for at least three minutes before moving on to the next stage.

Stage 3

The next exercise is designed to help you practise emptying your mind. This is best done while sitting. However, you can do this lying down, but resist the temptation to fall asleep.

Relax your body as we have learned to do previously, and close your eyes. Dismiss any thoughts that come into your mind. You can enhance this by saying to yourself that you are aiming to slow your mind down, and to have complete emptiness. At first, you may struggle to empty your mind. However, as you practise this, you will become better at it. An ideal scenario is to be able to empty your mind for five minutes. Realistically, unless you commit to and practise this regularly, this is not going to be achieved immediately. However, the very fact that we have a goal in mind then any form of mind quietening is going to benefit us going forward.

WHY SHOULD I BOTHER?

These exercises are very important to do. You may have a belief system that you are just one of these people that can't do certain things. People often have to validate something for themselves before a belief is changed. Anyone can do this, however, be aware of the mantra: "I just can't do this", and remember, argue for your weakness and it's yours. To quote one of my favourite quotes by Henry Ford:

"Whether you think you can, or think that you can't, you're right"

BREATHING

Breathing is an important aspect of changing our state. There is a link between the mind body connection and breathing. When we are stressed, we often have many thoughts going through our minds. In an earlier chapter, we learned that when the sympathetic nervous system is triggered in response to fear, breathing becomes shallower and quicker and occurs higher in the chest.

Compare this to when somebody is in a deep sleep. You will notice their breathing is slow and rhythmic and comes from the abdomen. If you have been on a relaxing holiday and you are lying down enjoying the sunshine, notice how your breathing is much slower, deeper, and from your abdomen.

We can take advantage of this difference in breathing patterns to help quieten our minds. Let's start with learning how to breathe from the diaphragm. The correct name is "diaphragm breathing" but let's call this "belly cord breathing" as it is easier to picture and remember. As you're breathing, notice where you're breathing from. In many cases, it will be from the upper part of your chest area, and not from your abdomen. To get into the habit of "diaphragm breathing" or "belly cord breathing" imagine that there is a cord attached to your belly button. Now imagine this cord is being pulled out, and with it, your lower abdomen. Breathing from our diaphragms causes us to relax. As this type of breathing is associated with relaxation, it's difficult to maintain the same levels of stress as the corresponding breathing pattern does not match.

Don't just take a couple of breaths and expect this to happen immediately. It takes a few minutes to have the proper effect. Do this for a few minutes to appreciate how it feels and notice how you start to relax more and more. If you can find a quiet place to sit or lie down so much the better.

We can expand on this and use a technique to calm ourselves in any situation. Let's explore this now.

A Boxing Match

Box breathing or square breathing is a technique that focuses on the difference in breath times between inhaling and exhaling. Box breathing keeps this very simple. The reason that I like this technique is that you can use this while out walking or moving around in an office area, and people won't know that you are doing it. Let's learn how to do this. You can practise this when you are walking or sitting down. When you are walking, it is easy because you can use your legs as a counting mechanism. If you're sitting down, simply tap your fingers either on the desk, a chair, a table or part of your body to help with the counting. Let's begin.

First, inhale from your abdomen using belly cord breaths for a count of four. You can either use four paces if you are walking or you can tap four times either on yourself or on an object nearby. Now hold that breath for a count of four. Now breathe all the way out for the count of four. Then pause for the count of four. The last part is the part that most people find the trickiest. However, with practise this will become easier. The second benefit of doing this is that while you are counting, you are unable to engage in negative thinking.

As you start doing this, you will start to experience physical relaxation, and with this mental relaxation, too.

Mindful Breathing

Another exercise that you can also try is mindful breathing. In this technique, you focus on paying close attention to the pattern of your breath. Become aware of what is happening as you are breathing. Notice the gentle rise and fall of your chest, and also notice that the air is warmer on the exhale compared to the inhale. Pay attention to as many feelings and sensations as you can while doing this.

SLEEP

Sleep deprivation can cause lethargy, and loss of willpower and self-control, together with motivational issues, leading to negativity and health related problems.

Sleep issues can be complex and are beyond the scope of this book, and the reader is advised to seek professional help if this is a problem. That being said, there are proven steps we can take to try to rectify the problem ourselves first. These are listed below:

1. Avoid going to bed on a full stomach and straight from work.
2. Include a wind down period before going to bed.
3. If you need to remember something for the next day, write it down.
4. Read a book before settling down to sleep.
5. Establish a routine and time for going to bed.
6. Avoid vigorous exercise before going to sleep.
7. Elevate your head about 5 inches or 10 cm.
8. Lavender calms the nervous system and bergamot and sandalwood oils have been shown to improve sleep quality in sixty four per cent of volunteers in a study.

9. A progressive relaxation method and belly cord breathing are effective for many people.

10. Avoid using mobile phones, laptops or computers for at least an hour before going to bed, as the blue light can act as a stimulant.

11. Avoid consuming too much caffeine during the day and particularly at night.

12. Walking and getting exercise during the day can assist with restful sleep.

13. Writing a gratitude journal improves sleep, according to a 2011 study published in Applied Psychology. It found that spending just fifteen minutes jotting down a few grateful sentiments before bed can assist you to sleep better, and for longer.

14. Lastly, a technique that works for me is to have a special speaker which is attached to my phone by a long cord and this is placed under my pillow. I listen to a seminar or talk that is low key and at a volume where I can just hear it. Using this, I find I fall asleep pretty quickly. This technique works well for insomnia too particularly, if you find yourself waking in the middle of the night.

The reader is advised to explore the latest findings if this is an issue, or to seek professional assistance.

Let's move on to our next chapter now, where we will explore the exciting topic of the Emotional Freedom Technique (EFT).

CHAPTER 19

Emotional Freedom Technique

The "Emotional freedom technique" (EFT), was developed by Gary Craig in the 1990s. It is also known as tapping. It is linked to the principles of acupuncture dating back over five thousand years. There is a substantial body of evidence showing its clinical effectiveness in a wide range of settings.

EFT tapping has roots in the 1970s. At the time, doctors began experimenting and stimulating acupressure points to help patients deal with phobias, fear and stress. Dr Roger Callahan was experimenting with this and he developed "Thought Field Therapy" (TFT). This involved many complicated tapping sequences. This was later simplified by Gary Craig under the name of the "Emotional Freedom Technique" (EFT).

The theory is based on the fact that our bodies have energy meridians, which are used in acupuncture where emotion and thoughts overlap. If the reader is interested, more information can be found by referring to the book, "Instant Emotional Healing", by Lambrou and Platt.

The idea of energy meridians covering the body may seem a hard concept for many people to accept. I have had first hand experience of the power of these energy meridians. I attended a training program where the instructor showed how to block the pain from a finger lock by simply touching a part of the body. The instructor then tapped another part of the body, resulting in people collapsing on the floor. I was highly sceptical and didn't believe this was possible, so I volunteered myself, only to find moments later I was lying on the floor as well. I can't explain what happened, but it worked.

I have the attitude that just because we can't explain something doesn't mean that it isn't useful or true. If it works, it works! Let's look at how the Emotional Freedom Technique (EFT) process works now.

Using EFT relies on feedback from participants. One scientific study found that EFT tapping had measurable results on the body. The participants benefited from lower heart rates and blood pressure together with lower levels of the stress hormone cortisol, after using the technique.

Research has confirmed the existence of the primo vascular system, which corresponds to many of the meridian points. In addition, functional magnetic resonance imaging (fMRI), studies have observed that EFT can calm the amygdala. The amygdala is triggered when the brain senses danger and with it the sympathetic nervous system, leading to the stress response being activated.

We have discovered the power of belief and the placebo. Some have explained the EFT technique as no more than a placebo. However, experiments have taken place in which researchers set up an experiment where a similar but not identical tapping technique was used. The result shows evidence that EFT tapping was more effective.

The point is largely irrelevant whether it is a placebo or not, but rather does it work? A lot of people have benefited from using the EFT tapping protocol. Many people swear by it. If it works for you, great. If not, simply try something else. We know from the research on placebos that if you believe that tapping yourself on the head with a pencil calms you, then who am I to argue? The point here is not to get involved in intellectual chess, but rather, are you getting the outcome that you want?

The EFT Process

The process itself is very simple and combines self-tapping with a phrase designed to focus the mind. It is very easy to do and can be used in almost any situation. Gary Craig has variations of his technique and longer versions of it. In this book, we are going to use the simple version, as it is easier to remember. The reader is referred to the work of Gary Craig to find out more if this is of interest.

Many people find after using the technique that they feel calmer and more positive about things, both in the short term and over a longer period.

THE TECHNIQUE

EFT tapping in 5 steps

Take a couple of deep breaths, breathing in from your diaphragm, using belly cord breathing as explained earlier.

For the EFT technique to be effective, you must first identify the issue or fear you have. This will be your focal point while you're tapping. Focusing on only one problem at a time is suggested to enhance the beneficial outcome.

Step 1. Identify the problem or issue

"Negative Thinking."

Step 2. Test the initial intensity

After identifying the problem or issue, set a benchmark level of intensity. Rate this on a scale from 0 to 10, with 10 being the worst or most difficult. The scale is based on the physical pain or discomfort that you are experiencing from the issue in focus. Establishing a benchmark enables progress to be monitored after having performed the complete EFT sequence. If the initial intensity was a "10" before tapping and is now a "5" after the tapping sequence, then we have a fifty per cent improvement.

3. Polarity reversal

Thought Field Therapy (TFT) surmised that blocks can prevent change even if a change is desired. These blocks are unconscious reversals in the polarity of our thoughts. Dr Roger Callahan discover that these reversals could be corrected by using a polarity reversal exercise. First, begin by saying the following:

"Even though I have (problem statement) I deeply and completely accept myself."

In this book, as we're looking at addressing negative thoughts, the statement could be:

"Even though I have negative thoughts, I deeply and completely accept myself."

Or

"Even though I engage in negative thinking, I deeply and completely accept myself."

Make this statement three times while rubbing in a circular motion a spot on your upper chest, which is located just below the collar bone on the left-hand side of the upper chest opposite the suprasternal notch. This spot feels a little more sensitive than the surrounding area (Fig.6).

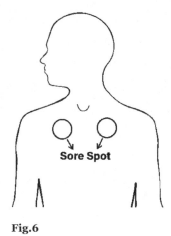

Fig.6

After you have said this three times and rubbed the spot, then begin the tapping sequence outlined below while saying the statement.

4. The sequence

To perform the EFT technique, tap each of the points shown in Fig.7 in numerical order while saying the phrase:

"Even though I have negative thoughts, I deeply and completely accept myself."

Or

"Even though I engage in negative thinking, I deeply and completely accept myself."

Start by tapping in the following sequence and use the fore and middle finger for a minimum of four taps. (Fig.7).

1. Top of the Head
2. Beginning of the Eyebrow
3. Side of the Eye
4. Under the Eye
5. Under the Nose
6. Chin Point
7. Beginning of the Collarbone
8. Under the Arm

Say the phrase while tapping each of the areas listed.

Step 5. Test the intensity again

Finally, measure and record the intensity of the issue on a "0 to 10" scale after completing the tapping sequence. This can be compared to the initial score to determine progress. If the level has not gone down to zero, repeat the exercise until either the score goes to zero or a plateau has been reached. At the time of writing, a link to Gary Craig demonstrating the sequence can be found at www.youtube.com/user/emofree.

EFT has been effectively used to treat war veterans and active military with Post Traumatic Stress Disorder (PTSD). In a 2013 study in Trusted Source, researchers studied the impact of EFT tapping on veterans with PTSD against those receiving standard care. EFT showed very positive results and has many strong advocates. If it works for you great, if not simply try another technique.

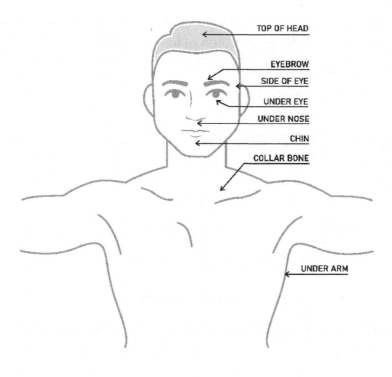

Fig.7

Let's now explore the fascinating and powerful world of neuro linguistic programming.

CHAPTER 20

Neuro Linguistic Programming (NLP)

N euro linguistic programming (NLP) evolved from the work carried out in the 1970s by Richard Bandler and John Grinder. It was developed by carefully modelling successful therapists and communicators, including Milton Erickson, Virginia Satir, Fritz Perls and others. Bandler and Grinder then developed models that ultimately became NLP. Modelling of excellence is now a common practise and is used in therapy, sports and the corporate world. It is incredibly powerful and can be used in any environment where people wish to change or alter their behaviour. There are always critics who try to intellectualise NLP. However, the evidence for its success is overwhelming and we are only concerned with "does it work?"

The "neuro" refers to the mind and the nervous systems, and "linguistic" refers to the language and the ways people create and express their experiences of the world. The "programming" refers to people's programming. In simple terms, it is the way people think, act and organise their experiences as they go about their lives. It can be thought of as software for the mind. NLP has some basic assumptions and these include:

1. Everyone has their own map of the world. NLP states that the map is not the territory, and it is subjective to each individual.
2. The ability to change the way that we process and experience something is more valuable than changing the content of the experience.
3. People already have all the resources inside them to make the change.
4. The mind and the body are part of the same system.
5. People make their best choices based on the information available to them.
6. There are no such things as failures, just outcomes. If something is not getting you the outcome you desire, then try something else.

At its core, NLP has a strong language basis and uses language patterns. When NLP is used in therapy, it focuses on the strategy that people use to organise their experiences. In other words, how do they do it?

If I am working with somebody and they say: "Public speaking makes them nervous", I then ask them how they do the "nervous part". There is often a puzzled look as they have never thought about this, and in many cases, they have to think really hard about it. I ask them what has to happen first. In the case of negative thinking, there is a trigger point or anchor, as we will come onto shortly. This trigger or anchor point could be a situation, a person, something imagined, a feeling, a smell, a sound, or an internal voice. Let's look at this trigger point or anchor in more detail now.

Anchors Away

I have an interest in lifting weights to keep fit and to help keep my strength up. Every year around December and January, in the UK on television, we have the opportunity to see the world's strongest man.

In 2017, Eddie Hall, from the UK, became the world's strongest man for the first time. After Eddie had won the competition in 2017, he was booked for a UK tour in 2018. My youngest son was nearly three at the time and had been fascinated with the program and with Eddie Hall. As part of the tour, he came to Edinburgh in Scotland where I live. I was lucky enough to have been given tickets as a present for my young son and I to go along. This was a big surprise for my son, as I knew he would love to meet Eddie.

On arrival, we had our picture taken and our book signed. Bedtime was fast approaching, and it was time for my young son to return home with his mother. I then entered the main hall and joined the other members of the audience and eagerly awaited the arrival of Eddie Hall. Eddie soon arrived and gave an excellent, informative, and humorous talk about his background, challenges, and achievements. After his talk, there was an opportunity to ask questions. I had been waiting for this opportunity, as I had a specific question in mind to ask him.

In addition to Eddie Hall being crowned the world's strongest man in 2017, he had also achieved the magnificent feat of being the first man to deadlift 500kg or half a ton. For those more familiar with the imperial measurement system, this is 1100 pounds. For anyone who does not frequent the gym, deadlifting 200kg (440 pounds) is very strong. Lifting 500kg (1100 pounds) is just unbelievable! This had previously been thought of as an impossible feat to achieve.

I remember watching this on TV and was amazed to see Eddie achieve the lift. Before the lift, Eddie seemed to be in a strange place mentally. He seemed to be in an unusual state before attempting to and successfully lifting the 500kg. At one point during the lift, it looked like Eddie's eyes were about to pop out and his nose started to bleed. In the end, he collapsed and needed oxygen to aid his recovery. Eddie goes into more detail about how this affected him in the days following the lift in his book. I was fascinated by how he had managed to achieve this lift, as there were other men, some of whom were bigger than him, who hadn't managed this.

Back at the event, my opportunity to find out more information was coming. I sat there, determined to make sure I asked my question. The previous questions concerned protein shakes, diet and exercise, and now it was my turn. I quickly seized the opportunity and put my hand up. The mic arrived, and the moment had come.

"Eddie, you guys are all big, strong guys. How much of what you do is mental and how much of what you do is physical?"

Eddie's reply was quite surprising. He informed us that, of course, you have to be big and strong, but over ninety per cent of what strongmen do is mental. He then said something quite surprising. He said that he couldn't have achieved the 500kg lift without the aid of a hypnotherapist. The hypnotherapist had told Eddie that he was to pinch the skin on his hand before attempting the lift. Doing this enabled him to get into the state that he needed. It wasn't an angry state, but it was a dark place. This is an example of what we call in NLP, anchoring.

Anchoring is common in everyday life, for example, when we hear a song, or when we smell a fragrance, and it reminds us of someone. Another example is when we refuse to go back to a restaurant where we had experienced a bad meal, even though it might have been five years ago, and the Chef has probably long since gone, together with the offending food.

Meeting with World's Strongest Man

Mouth Watering

Anchoring first came to prevalence from the work of Ivan Pavlov with his dogs. During the 1890s, Russian physiologist Ivan

Pavlov was researching salivation by dogs when being fed. Saliva flow was measured by inserting a small test tube into the cheek of each dog, and saliva was measured when the dogs were fed meat powder.

Pavlov predicted that the dogs would salivate when food was placed in front of them. However, what he observed was that the dogs would begin to salivate whenever they heard the footsteps of anyone who was bringing them the food. This was an important discovery in how we learn.

Pavlovian Conditioning

Pavlov started with the idea that some things are hard-wired into dogs that they do not need to learn. The ability to salivate when they see food being one of them. In behaviourist terms, food is an unconditioned stimulus and salivation is an unconditioned response. This means that it requires no learning. Unconditioned Stimulus (Food) leads to an Unconditioned Response (Salivate).

To explore this further, Pavlov created an experiment. In his experiment, he used metronomes, bells and lights as his neutral stimulus. Pavlov then began the conditioning procedure. He would start the metronome clicking just before he gave food to his dogs. This procedure was repeated until he just started the metronome clicking. As was expected, the sound of the clicking metronome on its own caused an increase in salivation. The association between the metronome, and the food had been established and the dog had learnt a new behaviour. This learnt behaviour is a "conditioned response", also known as a "Pavlovian response." For this association to occur and for learning to take place, the two stimuli have to be presented fairly close together in time (such as the metronome and the food). He called this the law of temporal contiguity.

Eddie's Anchor

When Eddie Hall had visited the hypnotherapist, he had learned a conditioned response. The hypnotherapist had helped Eddie to create the state that he wished to have. The desired state was then associated with a pinching of the skin on his hand. This generated the conditioned response or anchor. Just as Pavlov's dogs learnt to associate the sound of a metronome and bell with food, we can learn and bring back our desired state with an anchor. In Eddie's case, this was with a pinch of skin on the hand, but tapping a knuckle works too. It is best to have an anchor that is not too obvious, as we only want to select this when we want to use it.

If this method was effective enough to enable Eddie to lift a previously thought of as an impossible amount of weight, then just think of the power that this could have in your everyday life. We are now going to use a similar technique that the world's strongest man used to lift that seemingly impossible 500 kilogrammes or 1100 pounds weight.

Your Talent

If you engage in negative thinking and it affects you, and this is not from an illness or a mental disorder, then this is a real talent that you have. You have managed to make an experience that isn't real, appear as if it is real, and get your physiology, and your mind to react to it. Hypnotists call this a negative hallucination. You have used an anchor, just like Eddie, to do it.

I'm not being disrespectful or unkind here. This is actually a real skill to be able to use your imagination so vividly. This talent that you have is just being used in the wrong way. There is some really good news. If you are capable of imagining something negative happening to you or affecting you with such intensity, then it's perfectly possible to use this talent the other way around.

NLP gives us choices and taps into our internal resources to provide a solution. Remember, for something to exist, the opposite has to be present to bring it into existence. We spoke before about needing darkness to know what light is. We wouldn't know what negative thoughts were if there were no positive thoughts.

We are now going to do an exercise to show how this can be of benefit to you. For many of you, this will be a new experience. To get the maximum out of this, I want you to use your vivid imagination and engage as many of your senses in the following experience. It may help after you've read this to close your eyes and go through the exercise. The more that you can immerse yourself and become absorbed in it, the more successful it will be for you. If an experience doesn't come to mind, then simply play pretend or imagine that you are somebody else.

Your Personal Power Anchor

Recall a time in your life when you were at your very best. A time when you were at your most positive. You decided you were going to go for something, you went for it, and you achieved it. At this point, many people may experience negative thoughts by thinking: "I can't think of anything". If that's the case, simply make something up or imagine that you are somebody else.

Recall or imagine the experience as vividly as you can and see it as if through your own eyes. Make sure to adopt the same body position that you had in the real or imagined experience. The body position may be standing up straight with your head tilted slightly back, your feet wide apart a bit like the stance of a policeman, and perhaps with your hands behind your back like a James Bond master criminal. Make the recalled or imagined image as big as an IMAX screen, and see what you saw, hear what you heard, feel what you were feeling, and bring back any tastes or smells associated with the experience. Now make the colours brighter, make the images sharper and add movement to the image. Really experience it and step right into this and become a part of it. Imagine that there is a dial right in front of you that says experience enhancer. Turn it to full and notice how the feelings begin to intensify. As the feelings just begin to peak, either pinch some skin on your hand at a particular spot or tap one of your knuckles. If you are pinching your skin, it helps to do this in a place where you have a blemish, a freckle, or a mole so that you can go to the same spot each time. Remember to pinch the skin or tap the knuckle when the emotion is at its strongest as you recall the real or imagined memory. Now think about what you had for dinner last night.

Now repeat the process all over again. Keep doing this exercise a few more times until you have well and truly anchored the state that can be recalled with a pinch of the skin or tap of the knuckle. The degree to which you will achieve success will depend on your ability to fully absorb into the experience. We are using the same scientific principle that Pavlov used when experimenting with his dogs. Professional sports and business people use these techniques. In fact, you have been doing this to yourself with an anchor that starts the negative thinking process. It may even be an unconscious anchor that you are not even aware of. This time, we're going to use anchoring for positivity.

Congratulations, you now have a resource anchor. Keep practising this to strengthen the anchor.

SWISH PATTERN

The NLP Swish technique is a fast powerful method of altering how negative feelings, thoughts, worries and anxieties affect us. It's an easy, simple technique for swapping negative thoughts and emotions, and replacing them with powerful positive new images and feelings. Let's look at the steps to do this now. The key to success when using this technique is to immerse yourself in the experience and to be playful. If necessary, just pretend and exaggerate. It helps if you can close your eyes. Try and avoid negative thoughts such as this will never work. Many people have had great success with this method.

Step 1

In your mind create a large bright colourful picture of the way that you are acting and behaving when you are having negative thoughts. Make this undesired image very realistic but not to the point of causing anxiety or having a crippling effect. Take a few moments to do this, and when you have a clear picture in your mind, set this aside for the moment.

Step 2

Now create a picture, and think about how good you would look and how good it would feel to be rid of negative thinking in your life. Make this image as vivid and as enticing as possible. Add a compelling voice that reinforces how much you want it.

Step 3

Recall the first image of the undesired state as a large bright picture in your mind's eye, and recall the second picture of the desired state as a small dark image in the lower left-hand corner of the first image.

Step 4

Now very quickly make the small dark image of the desired state in the lower left hand corner of the big image, suddenly expand, and become the large bright image. At the same time have the undesired large bright image shrink suddenly to become the small dark image in the bottom left hand corner. As you do this, make the sound "swish".

Step 5

Now open your eyes and look around the room and think about what you had for dinner last night. Repeat the process quickly five times in a row, and make the sound "swish" each time. Make the last round of doing this really compelling by exploding the image of the undesired behaviour into fragments.

Step 6

Go ahead and test, and recall the old trigger memory. If this has been done correctly, you should not have the same negative feelings. If there are still some lingering negative feelings, go ahead and do another two to four rounds quickly. Then distract yourself by thinking about what you had for dinner last night, and then test again.

This should have worked by now. If you are still struggling with it keep practising this over the next couple of days. Make sure to bring in the emotional aspect of how good it would feel

173

to have eliminated negative thinking as you go about your daily life. This technique can be enhanced by using other methods and techniques that we will cover as we go through this book. If you are still struggling, don't worry. Simply try another method. We are not all the same and respond differently.

CHUNK DOWN

The term chunk down refers to getting more specific information. Language is important and is extremely powerful. We associate different feelings with different words. Try saying the word "relax" quietly and calmly a few times, and notice how you feel. Now read this text slowly and say it out aloud.

> *"As you are reading this text, and reading the words and seeing the shapes of the letters, really focus on these words. And as you carry on reading these words, and reading these sentences, the more you try not to think about it, the more you'll notice the increasing feeling of wanting to scratch."*

Did you feel the urge to scratch? If so, carry on and do it now. This passage is based on work by Derren Brown, the British illusionist, in his book, "Tricks of the Mind". If you are like most people and felt the desire to scratch, then this shows the power of words, and how we need to be careful with what we're saying and communicating when speaking.

We use language in an attempt to communicate our map of the world or our reality to somebody else. We also use language when we talk to ourselves. Language is powerful and shapes the thoughts of others. Think of the two words "freedom fighter" and "terrorist". In many instances, the outcome and actions are the same, but the perception is very different. One has a positive connotation and the other a negative one. Read these two phrases below to see the power of language.

I can't do it.

I can...,

not do it.

Did you spot the shift in meaning? We're going to explore how language affects our reality and how we can change it.

Chunking down or getting people to be more specific is used in therapy, as people tend to speak in generalisations. Common expressions that you may have heard people say are:

"I am stressed all the time."

"Nothing ever goes right for me."

"I never have any positive thoughts."

"I always fail at everything."

These statements often refer to an emotional component incorporated in a general language statement. When therapists hear these generalised statements, they are trained to probe further to gain more detail. We can do the same thing when we're talking to ourselves.

You may recall from Part 1 of the book, when we explored *"fast thinking system 1"* and *"slow thinking system 2"*, together with various cognitive biases, that logic very rarely plays a part in our decisions, despite what we believe to the contrary.

Let's look at an example.

"I am stressed all the time."

This statement on its own seems innocent enough. However, when explored in more detail, you can see that it is a massive generalisation. You could ask yourself about the validity of the statement. For example, are you constantly stressed, even when you're sleeping? The answer to this is clearly no, so this statement is simply incorrect. Let's look at another example:

"I never have any positive thoughts."

This statement is also a massive generalisation. It is very unlikely that somebody has never had a positive thought in their life. In fact, it is impossible to be negative all the time, and for the whole of your life. I don't think I have ever met a child who has never had a positive thought. Everybody has had a happy event happen to them at some point.

Get into the habit of chunking down. Start asking yourself more specific questions, and becoming aware of the generalisations that you are making. Becoming aware of these and any implied meanings that you attach will help you gain control over your negative thinking.

Be careful if you are asking yourself why you might feel that way. We are very good at rationalising our behaviour irrespective of how irrational it is. In NLP, we are more interested in the strategy that somebody uses. Let's explore that now.

WHAT'S YOUR STRATEGY?

Human beings have strategies or behavioural patterns that we use to achieve and do things. For example, we have a strategy for getting ready in the morning. There are sequences of events that take place. The same thing applies to negative thinking. There is a trigger point or an event that will start the process off.

When I was studying for my diploma in clinical hypnotherapy, CBT and NLP, I was part of a small group. The trainer demonstrated the use of strategies when working with someone who became anxious and nervous in front of people. The trainer asked the individual what has to happen first for them to become nervous. The individual looked somewhat puzzled. The trainer then asked: "Is it a memory or a sensation?" Then bit by bit the strategy for becoming nervous was uncovered, and the trainer used a technique to correct this.

Everything in life is a learning process. I don't know of anyone who suddenly wakes up one morning and is a world class tennis player. The neural connections have to be laid down. There are not many young children who exhibit negative thinking behaviours. In some cases, we can learn some actions very quickly. Some of these can be useful as we don't want to have to learn every day that putting our hands under boiling water, results in us getting scalded. Rapid learning usually has a strong emotional component linked to it.

NLP states we have a choice, and this is good news. We don't always have to go down the same path of behaviour. We created these paths so we can change them. Let me use a metaphor, or analogy to expand on this. Imagine that we have been used to walking through a field of corn, and there is a well-established path there. If we decide to make a new path, then the first time that we do this it would be hard work walking through the corn. The easiest choice is to choose the existing well-worn and well-trodden path. It is the line of least resistance. However, the more that we walk down the new path, then the more it becomes downtrodden, until eventually, it becomes just as easy to walk down as the original path.

We can give ourselves choices, we can either walk down the old negative path, or we can walk down the new positive path.

Delete that Program

A technique that I use when I have negative thoughts coming into my mind, is to say to myself: "Delete that program" and then swap the negative thoughts away from what I don't want, and change them to what I do want. I make the image big, bright and colourful, and attach movement together with seeing it through my own eyes. I also attach a pleasure emotion of how I will feel when I achieve that particular goal. This changing of focus immediately changes my state, in a method similar to the rapport building technique shown in the books, "Inside the Mind of Sales" and "How to Talk to Anybody".

We all get negative thoughts, and it is the degree and balance to which these occur that will ensure our success and happiness in our lives.

Dismantle the Inner Voice

This technique involves altering the submodalities of the components of our internal voice. I have used this technique numerous times with myself and others, and have found it to be very effective.

When we have negative self-talk, there is an internal voice that is talking to us. We all have self-talk which in many cases is negative self-talk. We often don't spend much time analysing this voice, but we are aware of it, and what it is saying to us. We have discussed before that it is useful to have thoughts critiquing our behaviour. However it is when this gets out of control and out of balance, that we have a problem.

Many people, when they have negative self-talk try to argue with this voice and they may say:

"No, I'm okay" or "I'm not a failure."

This tends not to work very well as it focuses on content, and in NLP we are more interested in the process.

Think about a time when you had a negative internal voice if you don't have one at the moment, saying negative things, or criticising you. What does that voice say to you? Where is that voice coming from? Can you point to where it is? For some people, the voice may be at the side or behind them. Is it coming from inside your head or outside your head? Is it close to your head, or further out? Is it straight on, or is it coming from the side, or is it at an angle?

Location, Location, Location

We can do various things with the spatial positioning of this voice. Experiment with moving the voice's location. If the voice is inside your head, then move it to the outside. Some people may have a voice inside their body at another location. We can also move the location of the voice from one side of the head to the other. Experiment with moving the voice further away from you. You may be in a room, and you may wish to place the voice at a distance away from you, as if coming from a certain object. Notice the effect that moving the voice has on your feelings about the message that it is conveying. Great, now return the voice to its original location.

Sound Check

We have looked at location however, there are other components that we may not have thought about before. We are going to experiment with this now. The delivery of a message vocally is very much dependent on the meaning that is conveyed. If somebody shouts aggressively:

"Get out of here!"

This has a totally different meaning compared to somebody saying the same thing in a jocular manner.

This time we're going to pay attention to how the voice sounds. Now listen to the words that the voice says. Is the voice talking to you in sentences? What is the meaning of the sentence? The essence of the sentence may be:

"I'm such a failure"

How does the voice sound? Is it a loud voice or is it quiet? Is it caring, or is it angry? Is it speaking quickly or slowly? Is it your voice, or is it somebody else's voice?

If the voice is a critical voice, change it to the voice of a ridiculous character. Perhaps you might want to make it sound like Mickey Mouse, or someone else who has a silly voice. Now, notice how the message feels? Have fun and play around with this.

LOOKING UP

A technique that you could use which will immediately interrupt your negative thinking is by using your eyes. We learned in Part One that people move their eyes in different positions to either access emotions, sounds, images, or to create them. Let's expand on this now.

Darting Eyes, Imagined or Real?

In most cases, if someone is right-handed, they will recall an image from a memory by looking up to the left. If someone is left-handed, the reverse occurs and they will look up to the right. If a right-handed person is creating an internal picture, then they look up to the right. The reverse occurs for left-handed people. (Fig.8)

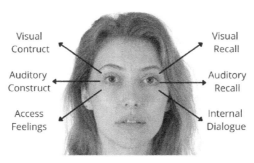

Visual Contruct
Visual Recall
Auditory Construct
Auditory Recall
Access Feelings
Internal Dialogue

Fig.8

I was observing this with my children. My daughter is left-handed, and she was fascinated to learn that her eyes moved differently to my eldest son, who is right-handed. My youngest son is also left-handed, and his eye movements follow those of a left-hander.

Start by watching people do this in everyday life to prove to yourself that this happens. Once you observe this and know that this is a phenomenon that exists, you can use eye movements to change your thinking.

Next time you are feeling down or are experiencing negative thoughts, look up and notice how difficult it is to keep having the negative emotion.

Project Recall

People recall their maps of the world differently. Let's use an example to illustrate this. Suppose that I was to ask you to think about your favourite holiday or vacation and ask you to describe it. Many people would simply recall an image and then describe it. However, do you recall the image as if you are in the memory and seeing it through your own eyes, which is called an "associated state", or are you looking at yourself in the image as if watching the memory like being in a movie theatre? The latter is called a "dissociated state". There is another state called the "double dissociated" state. This occurs when you are seeing yourself, watching yourself, in the memory, as if being in the projector room of the movie theatre, and watching yourself watching the movie. We have stronger emotions with an associated state than we do with a dissociated state, which is stronger than a double dissociated state.

There is a lot to recalling a memory. Is the image moving or is it stationary? Is it in colour or is it in black and white? How sharp is the image? Is it blurry or sharply in focus? If I was to ask you to draw a frame around the image with your hands, how big would it be? These variables represent sub modalities and we can change those, and in doing so, we can change the experience and our emotional attachment to it.

Let's experiment with this now. I want you to recall again your favourite holiday or vacation. Experience it as if being there, and recall the memory as if seeing it through your own eyes. Now recall any smells, tastes, or sounds associated with the image, and recall any feelings that you may have had at that time. Next, if the image was in black and white, make it in colour, and if it was stationary, make it move. Now make it sharper and brighter. Now expand the image as if you were expanding an image on an electronic device such as a phone or tablet, and make it as big as an IMAX screen. Now notice how you feel.

Now let's do the reverse. Take the image that you've recalled and make it stationary, black and white, duller and less sharp. Now step out of the image and imagine that you are sitting in a movie theatre watching the stationary black and white image. Make the image smaller and smaller, shrink it to the size of a postage stamp, and push it out into the distance. Take a moment to notice how you feel. Many people don't like this feeling, and want the original image and feeling back. When the image is shrunk, the corresponding emotions shrink too. You can play around with this and notice how your emotions change.

The point of this exercise is to show you that everybody has a strategy for laying down and recalling memories. It is important to realise the difference between an associated state, which is seeing something through your own eyes, and a dissociated state, which is seeing something as if you're in the movie theatre.

People who are negative thinkers are usually very good at dissociating themselves from the positive. They tend to be very good at associating with the negative. They are often very good at using their imagination and can re-live an experience as if seeing it through their own eyes vividly. What internal pictures do you make when thinking negatively? Are you in the experience, or watching from the movie theatre?

We can do a similar thing with the internal voice, particularly if you have a negative internal voice speaking to you, and we have explored this already.

Let's now move on to another powerful technique called "reframing".

REFRAMING

Reframing the Picture

As we know from earlier chapters, that reality is an illusion created by our brains in response to the data coming in through our primary senses. This means that we interpret and attach meaning to the data in different ways. For example, if a glass contains fifty per cent liquid and fifty per cent air, then we may describe the glass as half empty, but we can also describe it as half full. Changing the way that we look at things is called reframing. In the same way that the perception of a picture can be altered by changing the frame, then we can do the same by interpreting something or someone differently.

Notice the difference by merely changing the language. We can describe a situation as a "negative situation", or we can describe it as a "less than positive situation". I have heard trainers when speaking to their audience say:

"True or not true?"

Normally we are used to hearing, true or false. This may seem like a very minor point, however reframing plays a very important part in therapy work. When someone asked Thomas Edison, the inventor of the electric light bulb, how it felt to have conducted ten thousand experiments and to have failed, he famously replied:

"I have not failed. I've just found ten thousand ways that won't work."

If you read that statement again, notice the difference in emotion and feeling that you have when Thomas Edison reframed the experience. This is an important distinction in

NLP. There are no failures, just outcomes. If something isn't working, try something else.

Instead of saying I am miserable today, we can reframe this and say I have had happier days. This may seem like a minor point, but let's just look at the effect that language has on you. Whatever you do, I don't want you to think of a pink elephant, so please do not think of a pink elephant. I would imagine that you thought of the pink elephant, and then you deleted the image. That's the way the brain works. It has to, first of all, process the information, and then delete it.

If you use the word miserable, then this has a meaning attached to it. This meaning has a feeling associated with it. If you use the word "better", this has a meaning attached to it as well. By simply saying I have had better days, the brain has to first access its resources and process the word better, which has a positive connotation. By getting into the habit of changing the words and language that you choose to use, you will start to notice the effect that it has on you and others. Is eliminating negative thinking as simple as this? It could be, but this is unlikely in isolation. Everything that we can do to stack things in our favour, and to train our brain for positivity, is a good thing.

Understanding the power of language, which we explored in Chapter 11, including the work of Dr Masura Emoto, means that we can use a powerful phrase developed in the 1900s by Émile Coué to assist us.

"Every day, in every way, I am getting better and better."

Coué was a psychologist and pharmacist who believed that most mental and physical illnesses resulted from a person's thinking. He discovered that he could help the recovery of a patient simply by praising the effectiveness of the medicine to the patient when he gave it to them. Coué experimented with different phrases for different conditions, but this was his best known.

Using Reframing

As we have seen, NLP has at its core, there are no failures, just outcomes. It is the way you react to disappointments that will affect your wellbeing. Let's look at an example.

Years ago, there was a job that I applied for. I went for an interview and put my heart and soul into it. However, I didn't get the job. I remember being gutted that I hadn't been selected. Then, not long after, a better job came up with a better company. Had I got the job with the first company, I would have been out of work because not long after the interview, it was bought over. I hadn't failed to get the job. I had just made myself available for a better opportunity.

Politicians are past masters at the reframe, or spin, and many have "Spin Doctors" to put a positive view on less than desirable events. A politician may say: "Five soldiers were killed today, however, peace has now been restored to the area". This is an example of attaching something positive to a tragic event.

Learn to sharpen your awareness of the use of language and see how powerful it is. Let's now look at two more powerful techniques that we can incorporate as part of our journey to eliminate negative thinking namely, mindfulness and meditation.

CHAPTER 21

Mindfulness & Meditation

Mindfulness is a translation of the Indian word "Sati" which means "awareness, attention and remembering". It was originally developed in ancient times but Dr Jon Kabat-Zinn was the first to develop mindfulness for therapy.

Mindfulness means living and paying attention to the current moment. This is, after all, the only moment that we can live in. We can imagine the future and reminisce about the past, but we can only live in the present. In addition, it incorporates qualities like acceptance, curiosity and compassion. Mindfulness encourages responding to a current experience rather than reacting to thoughts. There is a temptation to judge and critique an experience as either good or bad. The ability to let go of judgments allows us to have a more balanced view of things and to be aware of the distortion, deletion and generalisation that occurs through our own personal filters. Mindfulness is useful as it starts the acceptance and observation process. It is not designed as a problem fixer.

Mindfulness Meditation

Mindfulness meditation is a particular type of meditation that's been well researched and tested in clinical settings. The idea isn't to clear your mind and think about nothing, but rather it is paying attention in a systematic way to whatever you decide to focus on. This may include awareness of your thoughts. Typically, this involves paying attention to one or more of a combination of breathing, the senses, the body, thoughts, and emotions. Thoughts have a significant impact on emotions and resultant decision making, as we discovered earlier in the book.

USING MINDFULNESS TECHNIQUES

It's very easy to get into habitual patterns of negative thinking, as discussed. Mindfulness encourages you to become aware of your thoughts, emotions, your actions and to question their validity.

Sensations

We discovered in earlier chapters that the conscious mind has limited capacity, and can only think about a few things at a time. We also discovered the importance of distraction in chapter 12, when we looked at the science of happiness. We know that we can move our awareness around, by simply paying attention to what we are experiencing through our senses. This means that we are less likely to focus on our negative thinking. This is very easy to do, as it simply means describing what we are experiencing at the moment. If walking down a road, we can describe the sounds, sensations, sights, smells and any touch or feel that we may be experiencing. By simply describing these to ourselves out aloud will automatically bring us into "now time". This prevents us from dwelling on the past or the future. This can be done in all sorts of situations. Remember, this is part of retraining our minds.

Curiosity

We can couple this by developing a natural curiosity about the things around us, and the other people we meet. In the author's earlier work, it was emphasised the importance of rapport building. This can be done using the "R + method", which is having an intense desire to get to know someone.

Breathing

Changes in breathing patterns are associated with different neurological states, and this was explored in Chapter 18. Becoming aware of any sensations and describing them, as you breathe, encourages you to be in the moment and not to dwell on negativity.

Hakalau

We can pay attention to our vision as we move our consciousness towards what we see. When stressed, vision goes from peripheral to foveal or tunnel vision. When relaxed, we have a much wider peripheral vision. As peripheral vision is associated with a state of relaxation, the nervous system can be tricked into being in a more relaxed state by engaging in peripheral vision, or as Huna practitioners call it, "Hakalau". The advantage of this method is that nobody knows that we are doing this, and it is less conspicuous than altering our breathing. Let's try this now.

Pick a point ahead in the distance. Look at that point and then defocus your eyes and start widening your vision. Imagination is important here. Expand your vision and try to see as much in the periphery or on either side of your vision as possible. The point that you had been focusing on will start to defocus, but that doesn't matter. Now try to see your ears on either side of your head as you expand your vision. Now imagine that you can see behind you. What will start to happen is that you will start to relax. It is not advisable to practise this if you're driving a car. While you are engaging in this exercise, it is very difficult to think about anything else as you're concentrating on widening your vision. This is useful to break patterns of negative thinking or anxiety.

Thought Awareness & Analysis

Box breathing and Hakalau will automatically help you relax and calm down. We learned that when people are stressed, the thinking brain shuts down, and we move more towards our primitive brains. Having become more relaxed, we can now start to analyse our thoughts and become aware of them. We can ask ourselves the following questions.

1. Is the thought a fact or an interpretation?
2. Is this all or nothing thinking?
3. Am I jumping to conclusions?
4. Am I biased to the negative and ignoring the positive?
5. Am I being unrealistic and seeking perfection?
6. Am I mind reading what other people are thinking?
7. Am I unfairly predicting the worst?
8. Am I judging too harshly?
9. Am I taking things too personally or literally?

Tips for Mindful Living

1. Spend some quiet time every day.
2. Enjoy the beauty of nature, and if possible, spend more time in natural surroundings, even if it is just a park.
3. Listen to and acknowledge your emotions.
4. Let go of negative emotions, acknowledge them and let them flow by.
5. Breathe deeply and smile whenever you can.
6. Develop an attitude of gratitude.

Gratitude is such an important practice that we will cover it in more detail in the next chapter. This can be used in conjunction with mindfulness techniques or on its own and can have some profound effects.

Don't get too caught up in the technicalities of mindfulness. It is more of an ethos, a change in behaviour and a sharpening of awareness than a technical skill. Let's dig deeper into gratitude now, and how this can benefit us.

CHAPTER 22

An Attitude of Gratitude

We looked at gratitude when looking at the science of happiness in chapter 12. We learned about its importance and how it affects wellbeing. Gratitude can be used as a form of reframing.

THE BENEFITS OF GRATITUDE

Gratitude improves physical health. Grateful people experience fewer aches and pains and report feeling healthier compared to ungrateful people, according to a 2012 study. Not surprisingly, grateful people are also more likely to take care of their health. They exercise more often and are more likely to attend regular check-ups, which is likely to contribute to further longevity.

Gratitude improves psychological health and reduces a multitude of toxic emotions, from envy and resentment to frustration and regret. Gratitude researcher, Robert Emmons, confirms that gratitude effectively increases happiness and reduces depression, together with enhancing empathy and reducing aggression.

According to a study in 2012 by the University of Kentucky, participants who ranked higher on gratitude scales were less likely to retaliate against others, even when given negative feedback. They experienced more sensitivity and empathy toward other people and were less focused on revenge. Grateful people sleep better. When a gratitude journal is completed, just before going to bed (as discussed in chapter 18), this has been shown to aid sleep.

The Science of Gratitude

Gratitude also improves self-esteem. A study, published in 2014 in the Journal of Applied Sport Psychology, found that gratitude increased athletes' self-esteem, an essential component of optimal performance. Other studies have shown that gratitude reduces social comparisons. Grateful people are less resentful toward people who have more money or better jobs. Being resentful of others is often a feature of low self-esteem. An attitude of gratitude allows for the appreciation of others' accomplishments.

Gratitude has also been shown to increase mental strength and reduce stress, and play a major role in overcoming trauma. A 2006 study, published in Behavior Research And Therapy, found that Vietnam War veterans who displayed higher levels of gratitude experienced lower rates of post-traumatic stress disorder. A 2003 study, published in the Journal of Personality and Social

Psychology, found that gratitude was a major contributor to resilience following the 9/11 attack on the US.

Acknowledging everything to be thankful for, even during the most difficult of times, helps foster resilience. We all have the ability and opportunity to cultivate gratitude. Rather than complaining about the things that we don't have or feel that we deserve, we can take a few moments to focus on all the things that we do have. Developing an "attitude of gratitude" is one of the simplest ways to improve your satisfaction with life.

Many of us focus on all the things that we don't have and miss out on the things that we do have. This leads often to a sense of dissatisfaction or emptiness. Gratitude is being appreciative of what we have, and not what we don't. Recent research shows that gratitude and appreciation give us access to higher brain states. Gratitude releases powerful feel-good neurotransmitters in the brain. Research from brain imaging studies shows that the reward centre of the brain lights up when we're feeling grateful.

THE POWER OF THE HEART

Most of us have been taught that the heart is constantly responding to "orders" sent by the brain as neural signals. However, the heart sends more signals to the brain than the brain sends to the heart. These heart signals have a significant effect on the brain and influence emotions as well as attention, perception, memory and problem solving.

Not only does the heart respond to the brain, but the brain continuously responds to the heart. The heart communicates with the brain in four major ways:

1. Neurologically (through the transmission of nerve impulses).
2. Biochemically (via hormones and neurotransmitters).
3. Biophysically (through pressure waves).
4. Energetically (through electromagnetic field interactions).

All these communication methods affect brain activity. Research from the Heartmath Institute shows that the messages that the heart sends to the brain also can affect performance. The heart is the most powerful source of electromagnetic energy in the human body, producing the largest rhythmic electromagnetic field of the body's organs. The heart's electrical field is about sixty times greater in amplitude than the electrical activity generated by the brain. Furthermore, the magnetic field produced by the heart is more than a hundred times greater in strength than the field generated by the brain. This can be detected up to three feet (one metre) away from the body and has been verified using SQUID-based magnetometers.

Evidence now supports the idea that a subtle, yet influential, electromagnetic, or "energetic" communication system operates just below our conscious level of awareness. The results of these experiments have concluded that the nervous system acts as a type of antenna, which is tuned io and responds to the magnetic fields produced by the hearts of other individuals.

It has been observed that this energetic communication ability can be enhanced, resulting in a much deeper level of nonverbal communication, understanding, and connection between people. This illustrates the importance of our state and its effect on our interaction with others. We can use this knowledge and use Heart Focus Breathing and Appreciation as developed by heartmath.org

Heart Focus Breathing & Gratitude

The following exercise is based on research by heartmath.org, and the reader is encouraged to explore this for more detail.

Make yourself comfortable with your legs and your arms uncrossed, either sitting up or lying down. Take a deep breath in from your abdomen using belly cord breathing. Hold it and then let it out with a sigh.

Now shift your focus to your heart and the space around it. Slowly take a deep breath in and continue to breathe in and out, both slowly and deeply. While breathing in and out, try to imagine your breath coming in through the heart, swirling around and then slowly going back out through your heart. Now add a positive heart feeling. Recall a time when you were filled with peacefulness and gratitude. Relive and tap into the emotions. Continue this heart-focused breathing in and out. The more that you can absorb yourself in the experience, then the more successful this will be.

Do this for a few minutes and notice how much better you feel. Do not do this while driving or when full attention is required, but it can be used almost anywhere and anytime. Getting into the habit of using this powerful technique will massively improve your thinking away from the negative.

Gratitude Journal

A gratitude journal enables us to write down the things that we are grateful for. There is something magical about writing down thoughts and goals. The very act of writing things down makes them clearer and enhances the thought process. Focusing on the things that we are grateful for changes our awareness and puts us into a different state. One of the most difficult things for most people is that they may feel like this is another thing that they have to remember to do.

The hardest thing, like beginning an exercise routine or starting a diet, is getting going and gaining inertia. However, we know how the brain works and the four stages of learning. To help encourage us to write a daily gratitude journal, it makes it easier if we can establish a set time to do this, similar to brushing our teeth before going to bed. If done often enough, then it becomes a habit. This does not mean that you cannot write down what you're grateful for at any time of the day. It is just that many of us forget. There are no hard and fast rules and you can do what is best for you. The advantage of using a gratitude journal before going to sleep is that it has been shown to assist with a better night's sleep, as discussed earlier.

Completing a gratitude journal has many positive benefits associated with it, including lowering stress levels, feeling calmer, and going to bed focusing on what's important rather than what isn't.

If you prefer to write in your gratitude journal at a different time, then a good idea is to set a reminder either as a calendar or as an alarm reminder. Some people prefer to write in a journal about the things that they are grateful for last thing at night. Others may prefer to complete it in the morning or at a set time during the day. It doesn't matter when you do it, as long as you do it if you want to see the benefits.

What Should I Write Down?

The conscious mind always likes to get in the way and to analyse and critique things and will want to know if we are doing the process correctly. A sample structured page is available here.www.eliminatenegativethinking.com
There is no set method for doing this. Simply write down as much or as little as you are grateful for. It doesn't mean being grateful for big items. It can be as simple as being healthy that day, or for your family, or your friends. Perhaps you've purchased something as a treat or achieved something. The magnitude is irrelevant. Simply write down how grateful you are. We are writing about how we feel about something and not the logic behind it.

Gratitude and appreciation are two incredibly powerful emotions. Start being grateful and appreciative for the people around you, the things that you experience and the things that you have attracted into your life. It's easy to do and will reap big benefits. It is one of the easiest things to do to train your mind for positivity.

A specially designed Gratitude/CBT Journal, is available at mybook.to/ENTJournal

CHAPTER 23

Conclusion

Negative thinking is something that affects many of us at different times and to different degrees. We have discovered that there is a bias towards negative thinking. Negative thinking on its own is not necessarily a bad thing, as it can be part of an evaluation process to assess the risk of something. It is when the seesaw of our thinking is out of balance and weighed down by negativity that issues arise. It is the degree, severity, and frequency of negative thoughts that can have debilitating effects.

In Part One of this book, we have covered how the brain and mind work, challenged accepted truths and conventional thinking and looked at the science behind this.

In Part Two, we looked at some of the most powerful methods, many of which are used by professionals when working with negative thinking. Not all of these methods on their own will work for each of us. We are all different and some will appeal to and be more effective to some than others.

When learning any new skill, practise makes perfect. Committing to using the tools shared in this book can not only transform your thinking and your life but also the lives of others around you. One of the best ways to learn any new skill is to break it down into small bite size chunks. One of the surest ways to achieve nothing is to try to achieve everything at once. Some of the techniques discussed may have more instant appeal than others. If you find that you're not getting the results that you want, simply move on and use another one. Remember, there are no failures, just outcomes. The techniques discussed have helped millions of people over the years, and they can help you too, as long as you make a commitment and practise them.

Remember to download the Rapid Learning Accelerator DTI audio that has been specially recorded for you. For many of you, this may be the only technique that you need. When listening to the audio, resist the temptation to critically analyse it. This audio works most effectively when you suspend belief. This is very much like when you are watching a movie in a movie theatre.

The fact that you have purchased this book shows that you are an action taker and are committed to seeking a solution. Don't just read this book and allow it to gather dust. Treat it as a working manual and refer to it frequently. Do this and notice how your life begins to change. If you wish to use a journal to help you, this is available here mybook.to/ENTJournal

Finally, we finish off where we started by returning to the quote at the beginning of the book. You can do it and I look forward to your success.

"There is nothing either good or bad, but thinking makes it so."

- William Shakespeare

See next page for your Bonus Audios

Get Your Complimentary

BONUS Rapid Learning Accelerator DTI Audio
&
BONUS Total Body Relaxation Audio

www.eliminatenegativethinking.com

Thank you for reading this book.

It would be enormously helpful if you would be kind enough to leave a review because it helps authors like me.

Many thanks, I really appreciate it.

Please leave a review here

Coaching, Training & Speaking Enquiries

www.power2mind.com

Please turn over to see the workbook and other publications

Other Books Available

Get Your "How To Eliminate Negative Thinking Journal"

Get "Body Language How to Read Any Body"

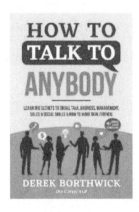

Get "How To Talk To Anybody"

Get "Inside the Mind of Sales"

REFERENCES

Alvarez, J. A., & Emory, E. (2006). Executive function and the frontal lobes: A meta-analytic review. Neuropsychology Review, 16(1), 17–42. https://doi.org/10.1007/s11065-006-9002-x

Backster, C., 2003. *Primary perception*. Anza: White rose millennium Press.

Bandler, R. (1976). *The structure of magic*. Palo Alto, CA: Science and Behavior Books.

Bandler, R., Grinder, J., & Andreas, S. (1990). *Frogs into princes: Neuro Linguistic Programming*. London: Eden Grove.

Bandler, R., Grinder, J., & Andreas, S. (1994). *Reframing: neuro-linguistic programming and the transformation of meaning*. Moab Utah: Real People Press.

Bandler, R., Grinder, J., & DeLozier, J. (1996). *Patterns of the hypnotic techniques of Milton H. Erickson, M.D.* Scotts Valley, CA: Grinder & Associates.

Bandler, R. (2008). *Richard Bandlers guide to trance-formation*. Deerfield Beach, FL: Health Communications, Inc.

Baumeister, R. F. (2012). Willpower. Penguin Books Ltd.

BBC. (n.d.). The placebo experiment: Can my brain cure my body? - media centre. BBC News. Retrieved July 16, 2022, from https://www.bbc.co.uk/mediacentre/proginfo/2018/40/the-placebo-experiment

Birdwhistell, R. L. (1971). *Kinesics and context: Essays on body-motion communication*. London.

Bolstad, R. (2011). *Resolve: a new model of therapy*. Carmarthen, Wales: Crown House Pub.

Bond, M. (2008). Review: Happiness by Ed Diener and Robert Biswas-Diener. New Scientist, 199(2675), 46. https://doi.org/10.1016/s0262-4079(08)62446-x

Borthwick, D., 2020. Inside the Mind of Sales. Derek Borthwick.Amazon

Borthwick, D., 2021. How to Read Any Body. Derek Borthwick.Amazon

Borthwick, D., 2022. How to Talk to Anybody. Derek Borthwick.Amazon

Brown, D. (2007). *Tricks of the mind*. London: Channel 4 Books.

Bruce Lipton https://www.brucelipton.com/category/topics/new-biology

Cannon, B. (2017). All about gratefulness with Robert A. Emmons, Phd. Eye on Psi Chi Magazine, 21(4), 10–13. https://doi.org/10.24839/1092-0803.eye21.4.10

Chabris, C. F., & Simons, D. J. (2010). The invisible gorilla: Thinking clearly in a world of illusions. HarperCollinsPublishers.

Chen, L. H., & Wu, C.-H. (2014). Gratitude enhances change in athletes' self-esteem: The moderating role of trust in coach. Journal of Applied Sport Psychology, 26(3), 349–362. https://doi.org/10.1080/10413200.2014.889255

Childre, D. L., Atkinson, M., McCraty, R., & Tomasino, D. (2001). *Science of the heart: exploring the role of the heart*. Boulder Creek, CA: HeartMath Research Center, Institute of HeartMath.

Cialdini, R. B. (2007). *Influence: the psychology of persuasion: Robert B. Cialdini*. New York: Collins.

Cialdini, R. B. (2018). *Pre-suasion: a revolutionary way to influence and persuade*. New York: Simon & Schuster Paperbacks.

Clance, P. R., & Imes, S. A. (1978). The imposter phenomenon in high achieving women: Dynamics and therapeutic intervention. Psychotherapy: Theory, Research & Practice, 15(3), 241–247. https://doi.org/10.1037/h0086006

Clark, B. C., Mahato, N. K., Nakazawa, M., Law, T. D., & Thomas, J. S. (2014). The power of the mind: the cortex as a critical determinant of muscle strength/weakness. *Journal of Neurophysiology, 112*(12), 3219–3226. doi: 10.1152/jn.00386.2014

Clark, L. V. (1960). Effect of Mental Practice on the Development of a Certain Motor Skill. *Research Quarterly. American Association for Health, Physical Education and Recreation, 31*(4), 560–569. doi: 10.1080/10671188.1960.10613109

Clond, M. (2016). Emotional Freedom Techniques for Anxiety. Journal of Nervous & Mental Disease, 204(5), 388–395. https://doi.org/10.1097/nmd.0000000000000483

Covey, S. R. (2016). *The 7 habits of highly effective people.* San Francisco, CA: FranklinCovey Co.

Cuddy, A. J. C., Schultz, S. J., & Fosse, N. E. (2018). P-Curving a More Comprehensive Body of Research on Postural Feedback Reveals Clear Evidential Value for Power-Posing Effects: Reply to Simmons and Simonsohn (2017). *Psychological Science, 29*(4), 656–666. doi: 10.1177/0956797617746749

Dantalion, J. (2008). *Mind Control Language Patterns.* Lieu de publication inconnu: Mind Control Publishing.

Dawson, R. (2014, October 14). The Secrets of Power Negotiating. Retrieved from https://www.audible.com/pd/The-Secrets-of-Power-Negotiating-Audiobook/B00NMQVS9G

Dyer, J., Cleary, L., McNeill, S., Ragsdale-Lowe, M., & Osland, C. (2016). The use of aromasticks to help with sleep problems: A patient experience survey. Complementary Therapies in Clinical Practice, 22, 51–58. https://doi.org/10.1016/j.ctcp.2015.12.006

Eagleman, D. (2012). *Incognito.* Rearsby: Clipper Large Print.

Eagleman, D., n.d. *Livewired.*

Elman, D. (1970). *Hypnotherapy.* Glendale, CA: Westwood Pub. Co.

Emmons, R. A., & McCullough, M. E. (2003). Counting blessings versus burdens: An experimental investigation of gratitude and subjective well-being in daily life. Journal of Personality and Social Psychology, 84(2), 377–389. https://doi.org/10.1037/0022-3514.84.2.377

Emoto, M., 2005. *The true power of water.* Hillsboro, Ore.: Beyond Words Pub.

Estabrooks, G. H. (1968). *Hypnotism.* New York: Dutton.

The Gary Craig Official EFT™ training centers. English (US). (n.d.). Retrieved July 11, 2022, from https://www.emofree.com/

Fox, M. E., & Lobo, M. K. (2019). The molecular and cellular mechanisms of depression: A focus on reward circuitry. Molecular Psychiatry, 24(12), 1798–1815. https://doi.org/10.1038/s41380-019-0415-3

Grinder, J., & Bandler, R. (1985). *Trance-formations: neuro-linguistic programming and the structure of hypnosis.* Moab: Real People Press.

Hall, E. (2018). *Strongman: my story.* London: Virgin Books.

Heller, S., & Steele, T. L. (2009). *Monsters & magical sticks: there's no such thing as hypnosis?* Tempe, AZ: Original Falcon Press.

Cedar Books. (1988). *How to win friends and influence people.* London.

Dalai Lama & Ekman, P. (2008). Emotional awareness: Overcoming the obstacles to psychological balance and compassion: A conversation between the Dalai Lama and Paul Ekman. New York, NY: Times Books

Ekman, P. (2003). Emotions revealed. New York, NY: Holt Paperbacks.

Hull, C. L. (1968). *Hypnosis and suggestibility An experimental approach*. New York: Appleton-Century-Crofts.

Jung, C. (2016). Psychological types. https://doi.org/10.4324/9781315512334

Kahneman, D. (2015). Thinking, fast and slow. Farrar, Straus and Giroux.

Kashdan, T. B., Uswatte, G., & Julian, T. (2005). Gratitude and hedonic and eudaimonic well-being in Vietnam War veterans. PsycEXTRA Dataset. https://doi.org/10.1037/e633942013-289

Kiley Hamlin, J., Wynn, K., & Bloom, P. (2010). Three-month-olds show a negativity bias in their social evaluations. Developmental Science, 13(6), 923–929. https://doi.org/10.1111/j.1467-7687.2010.00951.x

Kimbro, D. P., Hill, N., & Hill, N. (1997). *Think and grow rich: a Black choice*. New York: Fawcett Columbine.

Kindle, P. A. (2017). the upward spiral: Using neuroscience to reverse the course of depression, one small change at a time, by Alex Korb. Social Work in Mental Health, 16(1), 123–124. https://doi.org/10.1080/15332985.2017.1304496

Kirby, E. D., & Kaufer, D. (n.d.). Stress and adult neurogenesis in the mammalian central nervous system. Stress - From Molecules to Behavior, 71–91. https://doi.org/10.1002/9783527628346.ch5

Klaff, O. (2011). *Pitch anything: an innovative method for presenting, persuading and winning the deal*. New York, NY: McGraw-Hill.

Klopfer, B. (1957). Psychological Variables In Human Cancer. *Journal of Projective Techniques, 21*(4), 331–340. doi: 10.1080/08853126.1957.10380794

Knox, R. (2014, January 10). Half Of A Drug's Power Comes From Thinking It Will Work. Retrieved June 16, 2020, from https://www.npr.org/sections/health-shots/2014/01/10/261406721/half-a-drugs-power-comes-from-thinking-it-will-work

Koch, R. (1998). *80/20 Principle: the secret of achieving more with less. (Alternate title: Eighty-twenty principle)*. New York: Currency.

Kolenda, N. (2013). *Methods of persuasion: how to use psychology to influence human behavior*. Place of publication not identified: publisher not identified.

Krueger, W. H., Madison, D. L., & Pfeiffer, S. E. (1998). Neurochemical Research, 23(3), 421–426. https://doi.org/10.1023/a:1022426021173

K.S. LaBar & LeDoux, J.E. Emotional Learning Circuits in Animals and Humans. Handbook of Affective Sciences. Ed. R.J. Davidson, K. Scherer, & H.H. Goldsmith New York: Oxford University Press, 2003, pp. 52-65.

Lambrou, P. T., & Pratt, G. J. (2006). Instant emotional healing: Acupressure for the emotions. Broadway Books.

Ledochowski, I. (2003). *The deep trance training manual*. Carmarthen, Wales: Crown House Pub.

Lipton, B. H., PhD, Hedquist, J., & True, S. (2021). *The Biology of Belief: Unleashing the Power of Consciousness, Matter, and Miracles*. Sounds True.

Lorayne, H. (1979). *How to develop a super-power memory*. Wellingborough: A. Thomas.

Macknik, S. L., Martinez-Conde, S., & Blakeslee, S. (2012). *Sleights of mind: what the neuroscience of magic reveals about our brains*. London: Profile.

Maclean, P. D. (1988). Triune Brain. *Comparative Neuroscience and Neurobiology*, 126–128. doi: 10.1007/978-1-4899-6776-3_51

MacLeod, A. K., Coates, E., & Hetherton, J. (2007). Increasing well-being through teaching goal-setting and planning skills: Results of a brief intervention. Journal of Happiness Studies, 9(2), 185–196. https://doi.org/10.1007/s10902-007-9057-2

McGill, O. (1947). *The encyclopedia of genuine stage hypnotism*. Colon, MI: Abbotts Magic Novelty Co.

Michael H., M. I., C., G., & Volker. (2014, September 29). Neurobiological foundations of neurologic music therapy: rhythmic entrainment and the motor system.

Milgram, S. (1963). Behavioral study of obedience. *Journal of Abnormal and Social Psychology*, 67, 371-378.

Miller, G. A. (1956). The magical number seven, plus or minus two: some limits on our capacity for processing information. *Psychological Review*, *63*(2), 81–97. doi: 10.1037/h0043158

Müller-Lyer illusion. (2008). Wolfram Demonstrations Project. https://doi.org/10.3840/003252

Murphy, J. (2013). *The power of your subconscious mind, Dr. Joseph Murphy*. Place of publication not identified: Wildside Press.

Myrvold, Wayne, Marco Genovese, and Abner Shimony, "Bell's Theorem", *The Stanford Encyclopedia of Philosophy* (Fall 2021 Edition), Edward N. Zalta (ed.).

Navarro, J., & Karlins, M. (2015). *What every Body is saying: an ex-Fbi agents guide to speed-reading people*. New York, NY: Harper Collins.

Neal, D. T., Wood, W., & Quinn, J. M. (2006). Habits—a repeat performance. Current Directions in Psychological Science, 15(4), 198–202. https://doi.org/10.1111/j.1467-8721.2006.00435.x

Nijhout, H. F. (1990). Problems and paradigms: Metaphors and the role of genes in development. BioEssays, 12(9), 441–446. https://doi.org/10.1002/bies.950120908

Niven, D. (2005). 100 Simple Secrets of the Best Half of Life: What Scientists Have Learned and How You Can Use It (100 Simple Secrets, 5). HarperOne.

OBrien, D. (1994). *How to develop a perfect memory*. London: Headline.

Pantalon, M. PhD (2011). Instant Influence: How to Get Anyone to Do Anything--Fast (1st ed.). Little, Brown Spark.

Pascual-Leone, A., Nguyet, D., Cohen, L. G., Brasil-Neto, J. P., Cammarota, A., & Hallett, M. (1995). Modulation of muscle responses evoked by transcranial magnetic stimulation during the acquisition of new fine motor skills. *Journal of Neurophysiology*, *74*(3), 1037–1045. doi: 10.1152/jn.1995.74.3.1037

Pease, A. (1997). *How to read others thoughts by their gestures*. London: Sheldon.

Placebo: Cracking the code - top documentary films. (n.d.). Retrieved July 16, 2022, from https://topdocumentaryfilms.com/placebo-cracking-code/

Pulos, L. (2014, October 14). The Biology of Empowerment. Retrieved from https://www.audible.com/pd/The-Biology-of-Empowerment-Audiobook/B00O3I9V8M

Rossi, E. L. (1993). *The psychobiology of mind-body healing: new concepts of therapeutic hypnosis*. New York: Norton.

NLP power Dr. David Snyder. https://www.youtube.com/user/SanDiegoKarate

NLP power https://www.nlppower.com/product/killer-influence/

Raikov, V. L. (1975). Theoretical substantiation of Deep Hypnosis. American Journal of Clinical Hypnosis, 18(1), 23–27. https://doi.org/10.1080/00029157.1975.10403766

Realpeoplepress. (2010, July 14). NLP techniques - help with negative self talk - NLP ebook from Steve Andreas. YouTube. Retrieved July 11, 2022, from https://www.youtube.com/watch?v=JiVEfkUIuMI

Reik, W., & Walter, J. (2001). Genomic imprinting: Parental influence on the genome. Nature Reviews Genetics, 2(1), 21–32. https://doi.org/10.1038/35047554

Schmidt, H. (1970). A quantum mechanical random number generator for psi tests. Journal of Parapsychology, 34, 219-224.

Schmidt, H. (1970). Mental influence on random events. New Scientist & Science Journal, 50, 757-758.

Smoll, F. L., Smith, R. E., & Cumming, S. P. (2007). Effects of a motivational climate intervention for coaches on changes in young athletes' achievement goal orientations. Journal of Clinical Sport Psychology, 1(1), 23–46. https://doi.org/10.1123/jcsp.1.1.23

Syed, M. (2010). How champions are made. London: Fourth Estate.

Talbot, M. (1991). The holographic universe. London: Grafton Books. Endel Tulving. Elements of Episodic Memory. Oxford, Clarendon [U.A, 2007.

Tversky, A., & Kahneman, D. (1974). Judgment under Uncertainty: Heuristics and Biases. Science, 185(4157), 1124–1131. doi: 10.1126/science.185.4157.1124

Tibetan Buddhist monks meditation and science. tummo meditation. YouTube. (2011, February 6). Retrieved July 11, 2022, from https://youtu.be/XZUdtFu_hwI

Watson, J. B. (1913). Psychology as the behaviorist views it. Psychological Review, 20(2), 158–177. doi: 10.1037/h0074428

Welch, C. (2015). How the art of medicine makes the science more effective: becoming the medicine we practice. London: Singing Dragon.

Wendy A. Suzuki, Mónica I. Feliú-Mójer, Uri Hasson, Rachel Yehuda and Jean Mary Zarate Journal of Neuroscience 31 October 2018, JNEUROSCI.1942-18.2018

Wiseman, R. (2010). 59 Seconds: Change Your Life in Under a Minute (11/28/10 ed.). Anchor.

YouTube. (n.d.). Gary Craig's NewThink. YouTube. Retrieved July 11, 2022, from https://www.youtube.com/user/emofree

Youtube (2013, December 4). The case of ESP -- original, Uncut 1983 BBC film. https://www.youtube.com/watch?v=h2Gog3xMluA